AMERICAN INSTITUTE OF CERTIFIED PUBLIC ACCOUNTANTS

MW01140756

The CPA's Guide to
Long-Term
Care Planning

by Ronald A. Fatoullah, Esq., CELA
Harry S. Margolis, Esq.
Kenneth M. Coughlin
and ElderLawAnswers

1662-356

1 2 3 4 5 6 7 8 9 0 PP 0 9 8

ISBN 978-0-87051-716-7

Acknowledgements

A book such as *The CPA's Guide to Long-Term Care Planning* would not exist if it weren't for the help and guidance of many talented attorneys, assistants, editors and publishing professionals. Our state-specific information came to us from a large group of dedicated attorneys, including: Gregory L. Watt J.D., B.B.A.; Gene L. Osofsky, Esq; Dennis M. Sandoval; Joseph A. Dawson, Esq.; Marco D. Chayet, Esq.; Dawn R. Hewitt, Esq.; Paul T. Czepiga, JD, CELA, CPA, MBA; Henry Weatherby, JD, CLU, CHFC, CEBS; Ron M. Landsman, P.A.; Joseph S. Karp, CELA, Florida BAR Certified ElderLaw Specialist; Robert M. Morgan, JD, Adjunct Professor of Law at Florida Coastal School of Law; Stephanie L. Schneider, CELA; Ruthann P. Lacey, CELA; Peter C. Sisson, CELA; Susan M. Graham, CELA; Rick L. Law, Esq.; Martin W. Siemer; Brian K. Carroll, CELA; Randy Clinkscales; Bernard M. Faller; David R. Loveridge; P.A.; Richard K. Abraham; Valorie Leeb; Morris Klein, Attorney at Law; Hyman G. Darling, Esq.; Philip Moran P.C.; Carol Cioe Klyman; Christopher T. Lindsay; Long, Reher and Hanson, P.A.; Michael D. Weinraub, P.C.; Mary E. WanderPolo, CELA; Donald D. Vanarelli; Gerard J. Legato, Esq.; Neil T. Rimsky, JD, CELA; Brian Andrew Tully, JD, CELA, CSA, CLTC; Michael J. Millonig; Jerry D. Balentine, P.C.; Robert M. Slutsky, Esq.; Franchelle C. Millender, CELA; H. Clyde Farrell, CELA; Evan Farr, CELA, CEA; Rajiv Nagaich, J.D., C.I.C. Thank you all for your contributions to our book.

We would also like to thank Stacey Meshnick, Esq. and Debra Rosenfeld, Esq. for their assistance in editing this book; Celeste Panzarella for her help throughout the project; and to Danielle Beverly for her help shepherding all of the last minute changes and updates through. Thank you Martin Censor, Acquisitions Editor for getting us started on our journey to publication and thank you to the AICPA Specialized Publications team members: Heather O'Connor, Caitlyn Haase, Erin Valentine, Donovan Scott, and Trentypo, our Compositor.

About the Authors

Ronald A. Fatoullah

Ronald A. Fatoullah, Esq., CELA, is the managing attorney of Ronald Fatoullah & Associates, a law firm that concentrates in elder law, trusts and estates, Medicaid planning, probate, guardianship, and planning for individuals with disabilities. Mr. Fatoullah has been named one of the New York area's Best Lawyers in the Fields of Elder Law and Trusts and Estates for three years in a row, as published in New York Magazine for 2006, 2007, and 2008. Mr. Fatoullah recently received the prestigious Rose Kryzak Award for his "years of outstanding legal services to the senior population, and for bringing reassurance and peace of mind to their families and loved ones." In 2007, he also received the *Building Bridges Award* from AARP. Mr. Fatoullah serves on the Executive Committee of the Elder Law Section of the New York State Bar Association. He is the current Chair of the Legal Committee of the Alzheimer's Association, Long Island Chapter. He is also a co-founder and current board member of the Senior Umbrella Network of Queens, an organization of professionals that work with the senior population. Ronald Fatoullah & Associates has offices in Great Neck, Manhattan, Queens, Brooklyn and Cedarhurst, NY. The firm can be reached at 1-877-Elderlaw or 1-877-Estates.

Harry S. Margolis

Harry S. Margolis, Esq. founded Margolis & Associates, a four-lawyer Boston law firm, in 1987. He is a graduate of Swarthmore College and New York University School of Law. His practice concentrates on elder law, planning for individuals with disabilities, estate administration and guardianship. Mr. Margolis edits *The ElderLaw Report*, a monthly newsletter for elder law attorneys published by Aspen Law & Business. He also wrote the *ElderLaw Forms Manual* and served as founding editor of *The ElderLaw Portfolio Series*, both of which published by Aspen as well. Mr. Margolis is a Fellow of the National Academy of Elder Law Attorneys and of the American College of Trust and Estate Counsel. He has served on the adjunct faculty of Boston College Law School and is the founder and President of ElderLawAnswers.

Kenneth M. Coughlin

Kenneth M. Coughlin is editorial director of the Web sites ElderLawAnswers and Special Needs Answers. He has been the co-editor of *The ElderLaw Report* since 1992, and was an editor of *The ElderLaw Portfolio Series*. Before joining ElderLawAnswers, Mr. Coughlin was the editorial director of Faulkner & Gray's Healthcare Information Center, a publishing unit of Thomson Financial; the managing editor of *Insurance Review* magazine; and the managing editor of McGraw-Hill's Product Information Network.

ElderLawAnswers

Created by a nationwide network of attorneys, the Web site ElderLawAnswers provides consumers with the best information on the Internet about crucial legal issues facing seniors, as well as access to a network of highly qualified elder law attorneys nationwide. The information for consumers on the site includes primers on Medicaid, Medicare, estate planning, long-term care planning, and more. ElderLawAnswers attorneys have demonstrated a commitment to the field of elder law, and they benefit from the experience and expertise of their peers through Internet-based practice tools. You may contact ElderLawAnswers at: 260 West Exchange Street, Suite 004, Box #29, Providence, RI 02903. Phone: 1-866-267-0947. E-mail: support@elderlawanswers.com. Web site: www.elderlawanswers.com

David R. Okrent, CPA, Esq.

David Okrent is the principal owner of the Law Offices of David R. Okrent, which concentrates in the areas of Elder Law, Tax, Estate Planning, Estate Administration, and Asset Protection. Mr. Okrent has more than 21 years experience in both the legal and accounting fields and has received the Long Island Coalition for the Aging, Inc., "Man of Spirit" Award for his commitment to the field of aging. Mr. Okrent received his law degree from St. John's University School of Law, graduating Cum Laude. He received his B.S. degree in Accounting (also Cum Laude), from the School of Professional Accountancy at Long Island University. Mr. Okrent wrote Chapter 10, "Tax Issues," and can be reached at 33 Walt Whitman Road, Suite 137, Dix Hills, NY 11746; Telephone:1-631-427-4600; E-mail: dokrent@davidrokrentlaw.com.

Dennis Haber, Esq., CSA

Dennis Haber is Executive Vice President of Senior Funding Group and is an authority on reverse mortgages. His articles on reverse mortgage have been published in various national and local periodicals, including *New York Law Journal, Senior Market Advisor, New York Mortgage Press,* and *Elder Law Attorney*, to name a few . His groundbreaking book, *Piggy Bank Your Home for A Brighter Today & Tomorrow*, explains reverse mortgage concepts and is revolutionizing how families view reverse mortgages. In 2005, Mr. Haber submitted testimony to Congress on the Reverse Mortgages to Help America's Seniors Act, and he was also named to the Advisory Counsel for the largest reverse mortgage lender in the country. Mr. Haber contributed to Chapter 3, "Reverse Mortgages," and can be reached at Senior Funding Group, 247 West Old Country Road, Hicksville, NY 11801; Telephone: 1-516 570-5400 x208; Cell: 1-516 551 2189; E-mail denhaber@aol.com.

Table of Contents

Introduction

Accountants and CPAs render advice to their clients regarding income, gift, and estate taxes. However, when dealing with their elder clients, it is also important for practitioners to make certain these clients have a plan in place to pay for future long-term care needs.

Due to the lack of a national long-term health care program in the United States, your clients must rely on private payment, long-term care insurance, and government programs to cover the cost of such care. Unfortunately, many seniors cannot afford the cost of long-term care insurance, and most cannot afford to privately pay for the cost of their long-term care. Even if they could afford the insurance, many seniors are not medically eligible to purchase these policies because of a pre-existing illness such as Parkinson's or Alzheimer's. With that in mind, the nature of your advice to an aging client may change.

As a professional, you guide your clients through planning issues at multiple levels, but you can help them even further by being cognizant of the basic rules and regulations pertaining to governmental programs and other options for paying long-term care. This book is geared towards lawyers, CPAs, financial planners, and tax professionals with an overview of elder law issues and concerns, including advanced directives, Medicaid, Medicare, long-term care insurance, nursing home issues, and a multitude of other topics facing elderly clients and their loved ones.

Understanding Medicaid, Medicare and Social Security

The knowledge and understanding of Medicaid and Medicare law is crucial information you should have in order to confidently advise aging clients. In order to understand the current status of Medicaid and Medicare law, it is important to have an idea of the history of the respective programs. Medicare and Medicaid were established in 1965 in an effort to assist citizens over the age of 65. Medicare, Title XVIII of the Social Security Act, is the primary health insurance program for seniors. The Medicare program does not impose income or resource limits, and it is strictly a federal program with no state involvement. Medicare Part A (hospital coverage) is automatically available to those who have worked and are entitled to Social Security benefits and to disabled individuals under the age of 65 who have received monthly disability for 24 months.

Medicare Part B, which covers physician care and other medical expenses, is available to those who are eligible for Part A and for disabled people under the age of 65 receiving disability for a period of at least 24 months. Medicare Part B charges premiums that are automatically deducted from the recipients' Social Security checks.

Unlike Medicare, Medicaid (Title XIX of the Social Security Act), is a means-tested program. In other words, in order to be eligible, an individual's income and resources must fall within federal and state mandated levels. The entire Medicaid program was established in order to offer medical assistance to individuals who could not afford such care. Unfortunately, middle class seniors who cannot afford long-term care insurance must also rely on the Medicaid program.

Medicaid is funded by both the federal and state governments. The federal government establishes guidelines within which state laws must operate. The Social Security Act requires states to provide to the categorically needy under the Medicaid program the following at the very minimum: hospitalization, outpatient hospital, physician services, lab tests, x-rays, and home health care, both nursing and housekeeping. Most states, however, have very limited Medicaid funded home care programs. States are allowed but not mandated to provide additional services such as dental care, podiatrists, and optometrists.

From its inception, Medicaid included assistance for nursing home care. The need for long-term institutional care has increased with the aging of our population, making the program more crucial than ever.

The Supplemental Security Income Program (SSI), Title XVI of the Social Security Act, was established in 1972 to provide benefits to the poor, elders over age 65, the blind, and the disabled. Individuals whose income and resources are below mandated levels receive SSI payments. The federal government permitted states to continue using Medicaid standards that were in place prior to the implementation of SSI. Hence, in their Medicaid programs, some states use SSI methods and definitions while other states have retained earlier pre-SSI stricter standards.

What this Means for You and Your Clients

The ever-increasing middle class population continues to have a growing need for long-term health care coverage, and often has no choice but to rely on the Medicaid program. Frequently, middle class seniors look to the Medicaid program to preserve their assets that often has taken a lifetime to accumulate.

When establishing a plan for a senior, all possible means of payment for care must be considered. Alternatives to institutionalization present different financial ramifications for the client, and such ramifications affect the ultimate planning decisions made by the client.

Laws, rules, and regulations affecting seniors are in a constant state of flux, and the current climate is more restrictive than ever. The Deficit Reduction Act of 2005 (DRA), signed into law on February 8, 2006 by President Bush, reflects an attempt by the government to curtail Medicaid planning and minimize the protection of assets. As a result, it is more important than ever for the elder law practitioner to utilize whatever legal tools that are available, such as relevant fair hearings, regulations, unpublished cases, administrative directives, and agency memorandums, in order to advocate for her client. Proper planning by an elder law attorney can minimize the chance that an individual client and her family will not be impoverished by long-term health care costs.

Further, a tax professional may notice at some point in time that a client's mental capacity is beginning to diminish. We will address various options available to such an individual and her relatives, enabling the tax professional to point the client in the appropriate direction. Any tax professional who is unaware of the resources available to her client is at a tremendous disadvantage.

What this Book Covers

This book will help determine whether or not certain planning is appropriate for an individual client or her family.

Chapter 1: Advanced Directives. Advanced directives prepare clients for the possibility of incapacity through the appointment of agents who can make health care financial decisions when and if needed. A client's advance directives include, at minimum, two important estate planning instruments: a durable power of attorney and a healthcare proxy/living will. In this chapter, we'll discuss various options for clients and their family members given the possibility of a client's incapacity.

Chapter 2: Inheritance Planning. In addition to executing advance directives, including a durable power of attorney, health care proxy, and living will, it is time for the client to consider how to handle her estate and determine who will be the ultimate beneficiaries of her possessions and property assets. In this chapter, we'll discuss estate planning, taxation, and administration, and will also cover wills, trusts, and the impact inheritance planning can have on grandchildren.

Chapter 3: Reverse Mortgage. Reverse mortgages are a tool that some aging clients may want to utilize, especially if they own their home outright and want to stay in it for as long as is physically possible. Contributing author Dennis Haber provides the basics of reverse mortgages and helps you determine whether or not a reverse mortgage is right for your client.

Chapter 4: Medcaid & Medicaid Planning. For some clients a cost-benefit analysis may reveal that Medicaid planning is not beneficial or not the preferred option. Further, if a client is of a high net worth, Medicaid planning may be antithetical to a good estate tax plan. A great deal of Medicaid planning involves the participation of the individual's family. Therefore, it is essential to know the family dynamics as well as the financial well-being of family members who may be involved in a long-term care plan.

Chapter 5: Medicare. Medicare consists of four major programs: Part A, which covers hospital stays; Part B, which covers physician fees; Part C, which permits Medicare beneficiaries to receive their medical care from among a number of delivery options; and the recently-added Part D, which covers prescription medications. We'll discuss the various programs for Medicare as well as the topic of contesting Medicare decisions and Medigap policies.

Chapter 6: Long-Term Care Insurance. For some clients, long-term care insurance is a viable planning option. It is important for the tax professional to know when the purchase of long-term care insurance is appropriate for a client. And, if it is appropriate, what type of insurance should be purchased, what per diem benefit should be considered, how long the elimination period should be, etc.

Chapter 7: Nursing Home Issues. Most families try to care for loved ones at home for as long as (or longer than) possible, only accepting the inevitable when no other viable alternative is available. In this chapter, we will discuss some of the issues you will want to keep in mind as you advise clients on nursing home-related issues such as finding a nursing home, placement, and family disputes.

Chapter 8: Disability Planning. You want to reassure your client that she does have options if faced with a life-altering disability or if her spouse or child should face one. In this chapter, we'll discuss SSI and supplemental or special needs trusts and planning for a disabled child.

Chapter 9: Retirement Planning. State and federal government officials are slowly recognizing that home care can be more cost-effective than institutional care. This means that, depending on the state, financial or other assistance may be available for those who choose to remain in their homes despite declining capabilities. In this chapter, we will discuss some issues of home care and alternatives for out-of-home care.

Chapter 10: Tax Issues. With all the options your clients have to choose from in planning their long-term care, there are, of course, tax implications. David R. Okrent contributed this chapter, which focuses on tax issues that appear routinely in an elder law practice, plan, or both.

Conclusion: The Future of Long-Term Care Planning. In this conclusion, we offer up solutions to potential problems related to long-term care planning and provide you with a list of possibilities for your clients to explore.

Glossary. We've provided a glossary of eldercare terms made up of selections from the *Dictionary of Eldercare Terminology,*[1] 2nd edition, by Walter Feldesman. Dennis Haber also contributed to this glossary.

---

[1] It is available from National Information Services Corporation (Baltimore, MD). The entire dictionary is available for $28.00 + $6.50 S&H and can be ordered on-line from http://www.nisc.com/Frame/NISC_products-f.htm.

Companion CD-ROM. The DRA has significantly changed the way elder law attorneys advise clients regarding long-term care planning. States often apply the rules differently, but there are basic planning tools that the tax professional operating in all states should know about. On this companion CD-ROM, we've compiled a **State-by-State Listing** of the most pressing state-related information by expert elder law practitioners we could. Included in this list, you'll find Alabama, California, Colorado, Connecticut, District of Columbia, Florida, Georgia, Idaho, Illinois, Indiana, Kansas, Kentucky, Louisiana, Maryland, Massachusetts, Michigan, Minnesota, New Jersey, New York, Ohio, Oklahoma, Pennsylvania, South Carolina, Texas, Virginia, and Washington. If your state is not represented among this list, please check the ElderLaw Answers website, www.elderlawanswers.com, for information or contact an elder law expert in your state. We've also provided a list of **Resources** that includes calculators and checklists as well as a **Will Worksheet** for your convenience.

Advance Directives

1

The knowledge that we will eventually die is one of the things that seems to distinguish humans from other living beings. At the same time, no one likes to dwell on the prospect of his own death. But if a client postpones planning until it is too late, he runs the risk that his heirs may not receive the inheritance he wanted them to receive whether due to extra administration costs, unnecessary taxes, or in-fighting.

The issues facing elders who have missed their opportunities to plan include incapacity due to illness or dementia, not to mention death itself. Advanced directives prepare clients for the possibility of incapacity through the appointment of agents who can make health care financial decisions when and if needed.

A client's advance directives include, at minimum, two important estate planning instruments: a durable power of attorney and a medical directive/healthcare proxy or living will. The first is for managing property during the client's life, in case he is ever unable to do so himself. The second is for making medical decisions if the client becomes unable to do so.

The topics that we will discuss in this chapter include the following:

- Durable power of attorney
- Medical directives
- Capacity requirements
- Guardianship and conservatorship

Durable Power of Attorney

For most people, the durable power of attorney is the most important advance directive instrument—even more useful than a will. A power of attorney allows a client to appoint an attorney-in-fact to act in his place for financial purposes if he should become incapacitated.

In that case, the person a client chooses will be able to step in and fill the shoes of the principal to take care of his financial affairs. Without a durable power of attorney, no one has authority to act in the principal's place without the appointment of a conservator or guardian through court proceedings, which takes time and costs money. Furthermore, the judge may not choose the person the client would prefer. In addition, under a guardianship or conservatorship, the client's representative may have to seek court permission to take planning steps that he could implement immediately using a simple durable power of attorney.

A power of attorney may be limited or general. A limited power of attorney may give someone the right to sign a deed to property on a day when a client is out of town. Or it may allow someone to sign checks for him. A general power is comprehensive and gives the attorney-in-fact all the financial and legal powers and rights that an individual has himself.

Virtually all powers are durable, meaning they remain in effect even when the principal becomes incapacitated. Powers of attorney may also be effective immediately or springing, which means the powers are only valid at the time when the individual becomes incapacitated. In such cases, it is very important that the standard for determining incapacity and triggering the power of attorney be clearly laid out in the document itself.

Attorneys report that their clients are experiencing increasing difficulty in getting banks or other financial institutions to recognize the authority of an agent under a durable power of attorney. A certain amount of caution on the part of financial institutions is understandable: When someone steps forward claiming to represent the account holder, the financial institution wants to verify that the attorney-in-fact indeed has the authority to act for the principal. Still, some institutions go overboard, for example, requiring that the attorney-in-fact indemnify them against any loss. State statutes have different provisions that apply to powers of attorney. Some states require a bank to accept a power of attorney. Some statutory forms indemnify the banks.

Many banks or other financial institutions have their own standard power of attorney forms. To avoid problems, a client may want to execute such forms offered by the institutions with which he has accounts. In addition, many attorneys counsel their clients to create living trusts in part to avoid this sort of problem with powers of attorney.

While a client should seriously consider executing a durable power of attorney, if he does not have someone he trusts, it may be more appropriate to have the appropriate court overseeing the handling of his affairs through a guardianship or conservatorship. In that case, the client may execute a limited durable power of attorney simply nominating the person he wants to serve as his conservator or guardian. Most states require the court to respect his nomination except for good cause or disqualification.

As you counsel clients about appointing an attorney-in-fact, you may also want to share the following facts with them:

Can the attorney-in-fact be held liable for his actions? Yes, but only if the attorney-in-fact acts with willful misconduct or gross negligence. If the attorney-in-fact does his best and keeps the principal's interests in mind as the basis of his actions, the attorney-in-fact will not incur any liability.

What if there is more than one attorney-in-fact? While one can appoint attorneys-in-fact to act jointly, in most cases, when there are multiple attorneys-in-fact, they are appointed severally, meaning that they can each act independently of one another. Nevertheless, it is important for them to communicate with one another to make certain that their actions are consistent. If they disagree or take conflicting steps, it can create a serious problem. The only solution may be a guardianship or conservatorship under which a court would choose one of them, both of them, or someone else to make the decisions.

Can the attorney-in-fact be compensated for his work? Yes. In general, the attorney-in-fact is entitled to reasonable compensation for his services. However, in most cases, the attorney-in-fact is a family member and does not expect to be paid. If an attorney-in-fact would like to be paid, it is best that he discuss this with the principal, agree on a reasonable rate of payment, and put that agreement in writing. That is the only way to avoid misunderstandings in the future.

Medical Directives

Medical science has created many miracles, among them the technology to keep patients alive longer, sometimes seemingly indefinitely. As a result of many well-publicized *right-to-die* cases, states have made it possible for individuals to give detailed instructions regarding the kind of care they would like to receive should they become terminally ill or are in a permanently unconscious state. These instructions fall under the general category of *health care decision making*. Depending on the state in which a client lives, this may take the form of a health care proxy, a medical directive, or a living will.

Both a health care proxy and a durable power of attorney for health care designate someone to make health care decisions if the client is unable to do so. A living will instructs a health care provider to withdraw life support if the client is terminally ill or in a vegetative state. A broader medical directive may include the terms of a living will, but will also provide instructions if the client is in a less severe state of health, but is still unable to direct his health care himself.

The Health Care Proxy or Durable Power of Attorney for Health Care

If an individual becomes incapacitated, it is important that someone has the legal authority to communicate that person's wishes concerning medical treatment. Similar to a financial power of attorney, a health care proxy or power of attorney allows an individual to appoint someone else to act as an agent, but for medical rather than financial decisions. The health care proxy is a document executed by a competent person (the principal) giving another person (the agent) the authority to make health care decisions for the principal if he is unable to communicate such decisions. A health care proxy is especially important to have if an individual and his family members disagree about treatment.

In general, a health care proxy takes effect only when the principal requires medical treatment and a physician determines that he is unable to communicate his wishes concerning treatment. How this works can depend on the laws of the particular state and the terms of the health care proxy itself. If the principal later becomes able to express his own wishes, the health care proxy will have no effect.

Appointing an Agent

Since the agent will have the authority to make medical decisions in the event the principal is unable to make such decisions for himself, the agent should be a family member or friend that the principal trusts to follow his instructions. Before executing a health care proxy, the principal should talk to the person whom he chooses to name as the agent about his wishes concerning medical decisions, especially life-sustaining treatment.

Once the health care proxy is drawn up, the agent should retain the original document. The principal should have a copy and the principal's physician should keep a copy with that individual's medical records.

Health care proxies are generally included in any estate plan prepared by an attorney who is skilled and experienced in elder law matters. Many hospitals and nursing homes also provide forms, as do some public agencies.

The Medical Directive Document

Most practitioners recommend that a medical directive accompany a health care proxy. Such directives provide the agent with specific instructions on the principal's wishes regarding care. A medical directive can be included in the health care proxy, or it can be a separate document. It may contain directions to refuse or remove life support in the event the principal is in a coma or a vegetative state, or it may provide instructions to use all efforts to keep the principal alive, no matter what the circumstances. Medical directives can also provide the agent with guidance on what decisions to make in less serious situations.

Living Wills

Living wills are documents that give instructions regarding treatment if an individual becomes terminally ill or is in a persistent vegetative state and is unable to communicate his own instructions. The living will states under what conditions life-sustaining treatment should be terminated. If an individual would like to avoid life-sustaining treatment when it would be hopeless, he needs to execute a living will. Like a health care proxy, a living will takes effect only upon a person's incapacity. Also, a living will is not irrevocable; an individual can always revoke it at a later date if he wishes to do so.

A living will, however, is not necessarily a substitute for a health care proxy or a broader medical directive. It simply dictates the withdrawal of life support in instances of terminal illness, coma, or a persistent vegetative state.

HIPPA Release

With passage of the Health Insurance Portability and Accountability Act of 1996, health care providers have been strictly limited in terms of divulging information to persons other than the patient himself. They can only do so with written authorization in the form of a release. This may be a freestanding document, or it may be incorporated into a health care proxy or durable powers of attorney.

Capacity Requirements

Proper execution of a legal instrument requires that the person signing have sufficient mental *capacity* to understand the implications of the document. While most people speak of legal "capacity" or "competence" as a rigid black line—either the person has it or doesn't—in fact, it can be variable depending on the function for which capacity is required.

One side of the capacity equation involves the client's abilities, which may change from day to day (or even during the day), depending on the course of the illness, fatigue, and effects of medication. On the other side, greater understanding is required for some legal documents than for others. For instance, the capacity required for entering into a contract is higher than that required to execute a will.

The standard definition of capacity for wills has been aptly summed up by the Massachusetts Supreme Judicial Court:

> Testamentary capacity requires ability on the part of the testator to understand and carry in mind, in a general way, the nature and situation of his property and his relations to those persons who would naturally have some claim to his remembrance. It requires freedom from delusion, which is the effect of disease or weakness and which might influence the disposition of his property. And it requires ability at the time of execution of the alleged will to comprehend the nature of the act of making a will.

Massachusetts has a relatively low threshold, meaning that signing a will does not require a great deal of capacity. The fact that the next day the testator does not remember the will signing and is not sufficiently "with it" to execute a will then does not invalidate the will if he understood it when he signed it.

The standard of capacity with respect to durable powers of attorney varies from jurisdiction to jurisdiction. Some practitioners argue that this threshold can be quite low. The client need only know that he trusts the attorney-in-fact to manage his financial affairs. Others argue that since the attorney-in-fact generally has the right to enter into contracts on behalf of the principal, the principal should have capacity to enter into contracts as well. The threshold for entering into contracts is fairly high.

The standards for entering into a contract are different because the individual must know not only the nature of his property and the person with whom he is dealing, but also the broader context of the market in which he is agreeing to buy or sell services or property. In *Farnum v. Silvano* in 1989, the Massachusetts Appeals Court reversed the sale of a home by a 90-year-old woman suffering from organic brain syndrome. The sale was for half of the house's market value. The court contrasted competency to sell property with the capacity to make a will, the latter requiring only understanding at the time of executing the will:

> Competency to enter into a contract presupposes something more than a transient surge of lucidity. It requires the ability to comprehend the nature and quality of the transaction, together with an understanding of what is "going on," but an ability to comprehend the nature and quality of the transaction, together with an understanding of its significance and consequences.

As a practical matter, in assessing a client's capacity to execute a legal document, attorneys generally ask the question "Is anyone going to challenge this transaction?" If a client of questionable capacity executes a will leaving his estate to his wife, and then to his children if his wife does not survive him, it's unlikely to be challenged. If, on the other hand, he executes a will giving his estate entirely to one daughter with nothing passing to his wife or other children, the likelihood of challenge is greater.

While the standards may seem clear, applying them to particular clients may be difficult. The fact that a client does not know the year or the name of the president may mean he does not have capacity to enter into a contract, but not necessarily that he cannot execute a will or durable power of attorney. The determination mixes medical, psychological, and legal judgments. It must be made by the attorney (or a judge, in the case of guardianship and conservatorship determinations) based on information gleaned from the attorney's interactions with the client, from other sources such as family members and social workers, and, if necessary, from medical personnel. Doctors and psychiatrists themselves cannot make a determination as to whether an individual has capacity to undertake a legal commitment. But they can provide a professional evaluation of the person that will help an attorney make this decision.

Guardianship and Conservatorship

Every adult is assumed to be capable of making his own decisions unless a court determines otherwise. If an adult becomes incapable of making responsible decisions due to a mental disability, the court may appoint a substitute decision maker, often called a *guardian*, but in some states called a *conservator* or other term. Guardianship is a legal relationship between a competent adult (the guardian) and a person who, because of incapacity, is no longer able to take care of his own affairs (the ward or incapacitated person).

Generally, when someone is appointed guardian for another, that guardian "stands in the shoes" of the ward and is given the legal responsibility to make all decisions for him, whether financial, medical, or personal. (In some states, this is known as *conservatorship*; in others, conservatorship refers only to financial responsibility.) While guardianship takes away the ward's right to act for himself, the guardian has a fiduciary responsibility to act in the ward's interest and take actions that he would if able to do so, known as a *substituted judgment*. This means that the guardian should take direction from the ward to the extent that the ward is able to express himself.

Most states allow for *limited guardianships*, where the court determines what specific rights will be transferred from the ward to the guardian. Unfortunately, in practice most courts do not take the time to craft a guardianship to the specific needs of the ward. It's easier for all the parties but the ward to request a more comprehensive guardianship. Anyone appointed the unlimited or *plenary* guardian for a parent (or anyone else) should still seek that person's participation in all decisions in order to help the ward retain his dignity and sense of self despite the guardianship appointment.

Incapacity

The standard under which a person is deemed to require a guardian differs from state to state. In some states the standards are different, depending on whether a complete guardianship or a conservatorship over finances only is being sought. Generally a person is judged to be in need of guardianship when he shows a lack of capacity to make responsible decisions. A person cannot be declared incompetent simply because he makes irresponsible or foolish decisions—only if the person is shown to lack capacity to make sound decisions. For example, a person may not be declared incompetent simply because he spends money in ways that seem odd to someone else. Also, a developmental disability or mental illness is not, by itself, enough to declare a person incompetent.

Process

In most states, anyone interested in the proposed ward's well-being can request a guardianship. An attorney is usually retained to file a petition for a hearing in the probate court in the proposed ward's county of residence. Protections for the proposed ward vary greatly from state to state, with some simply requiring that notice of the proceeding be provided and others requiring the proposed ward's presence at the hearing. The proposed ward is usually entitled to legal representation at the hearing, and the court will appoint an attorney if the allegedly incapacitated person cannot afford a lawyer.

At the hearing, the court attempts to determine if the proposed ward is incapacitated and, if so, to what extent the individual requires assistance. If the court determines that the proposed ward is indeed incapacitated, then the court decides if the person seeking the role of guardian will be a responsible guardian.

A guardian can be any competent adult—the ward's spouse, another family member, a friend, a neighbor, or a professional guardian (an unrelated person who has received special training). A competent individual may nominate a proposed guardian through a durable power of attorney in case he ever needs a guardian.

The guardian need not be a person at all. In many states, it can be a non-profit agency or a public or private corporation. If a suitable guardian cannot be found for an incapacitated person, courts in some states can appoint a public guardian, a publicly financed agency that serves this purpose. In naming someone to serve as a guardian, courts give first consideration to those who play a significant role in the ward's life—people who are both aware of and sensitive to the ward's needs and preferences. If two individuals wish to share guardianship duties, courts can name co-guardians.

Reporting Requirements

Courts often give guardians broad authority to manage the ward's affairs. In addition to lacking the power to decide how money is spent or managed, where to live, and what medical care he should receive, wards also may not have the right to vote, marry or divorce, or carry a driver's license. Guardians are expected to act in the best interests of the ward, but given the guardian's often broad authority, there is the potential for abuse. For this reason, courts hold guardians accountable for their actions to ensure that they do not take advantage of or neglect the ward.

The guardian of the property inventories the ward's property, invests the ward's funds so that they can be used for the ward's support, and files regular, detailed reports with the court. A guardian of the property also must obtain court approval for certain financial transactions. Guardians must file an annual account of how they have handled the ward's finances. In some states, guardians must also give an annual report on the ward's status. Guardians must offer proof that they made adequate residential arrangements for the ward, that they provided sufficient health care and treatment services, and that they made available educational and training programs, as needed. Guardians who cannot prove that they have adequately cared for the ward may be removed and replaced by another guardian.

Alternatives

Because guardianship involves a profound loss of freedom and dignity, state laws require that guardianship be imposed only when less restrictive alternatives have been tried and proven to be ineffective. Less restrictive alternatives that should be considered before pursuing guardianship include the following:

- **Power of Attorney.** As discussed previously, a power of attorney is the grant of legal rights and powers by a person (the principal) to another (the agent or attorney-in-fact). The attorney-in-fact, in effect, stands in the shoes of the principal and acts for him on financial, business, or other matters. In most cases, even when the power of attorney is immediately effective, the principal does not intend for it to be used unless and until he becomes incapacitated.
- **Representative or Protective Payee.** A representative or protective payee is a person appointed to manage Social Security, Veterans' Administration, Railroad Retirement, welfare, or other state or federal benefits or entitlement program payments on behalf of an individual.
- **Conservatorship.** In some states, this proceeding can be voluntary, where the person needing assistance with finances petitions the probate court to appoint a specific person (the conservator) to manage his financial affairs. The court must determine that the conservatee is unable to manage his own financial affairs, but nevertheless has the capacity to make the decision to have a conservator appointed to handle his affairs.
- **Revocable trust.** A revocable or *living* trust can be set up to hold an older person's assets, with a relative, friend, or financial institution serving as trustee. Alternatively, the older person can be a co-trustee of the trust with another individual who will take over the duties of trustee should the older person become incapacitated.

Inheritance Planning

2

In addition to executing advance directives, including a durable power of attorney, health care proxy, and living will, it is time for the client to consider how to handle her estate and determine who will be the ultimate beneficiaries of her possessions and property assets.

The topics that we will discuss in this chapter include the following:

- Estate planning
- Estate taxation
- Estate administration
- Wills
- Trusts
- Grandchildren

Estate Planning

An *estate* is composed of everything an individual owns, including bank accounts, stock, real estate, motor vehicles, jewelry, household furniture, retirement plans, and life insurance. An estate plan is the means by which a client passes her estate to the next generation. This can be accomplished through a variety of instruments. Most retirement plans and life insurance policies pass to whoever is named as beneficiary. Property that is jointly owned passes to the surviving joint owner by operation of law. Trust assets are distributed alone as provided for by the terms of the trust.

Only property that is held in the name of the decedent alone falls under the instructions laid out in the decedent's will. This is known as *probate* property and all other property is known as *non-probate* property.

If a client does not have a will, such probate property passes under the laws of *intestacy* set out in state law. In general, those rules provide that the client's property will be divided among her closest family members. Problems often arise when people do not coordinate all of these various methods of passing on their estate. The will may say to divide everything equally among the decedent's children, but if she owns an account jointly with another child "for the sake of convenience," there could be a conflict about whether that account should be put back in the pool with the rest of her property.

One of the most important aspects of a will is that it names an executor or personal representative to handle the probate of the decedent's estate. Litigation can develop simply because family members cannot agree on who should take on this role. For those with small children, the will is indispensable because it permits the parents to appoint a guardian in case both parents pass away. It also permits them to choose a trustee to manage their estate assets for the benefit of their children. This person may or may not be the same as the guardian.

For many individuals, especially those with smaller estates, the most important document to have during one's lifetime is a durable power of attorney, which was discussed in Chapter 1, "Advanced Directives." Through a durable power of attorney, an individual can appoint someone to handle her finances in the event that she becomes incapacitated and is unable to manage her affairs herself. Similar to a durable power of attorney, a health care proxy appoints someone a client trusts to make medical decisions for her in the event of her incapacity. While a will protects her estate after her demise, a durable power of attorney and health care proxy protect an individual while she's still alive.

Some individuals may wonder if their joint bank and brokerage accounts eliminate the need to establish beneficiaries within a will. Unless a client has only one child, relying solely on joint bank and retirement accounts as a means for money to pass along to a child is inadvisable. It is impossible to keep separate accounts for more than one child equal. This is especially true if a client should become incapacitated and can no longer be in control over the accounts. Trying to save a few dollars by managing an estate in this fashion runs the strong risk of causing discord among family members for generations to come. In addition, such an arrangement does not take into account what happens if one of the named beneficiaries or joint holders on the account predeceases the client. Individuals should be discouraged from relying solely on handling their estate administration through the naming of account beneficiaries.

While an individual can purchase software that produces most of the estate planning documents an attorney will prepare, this is not advisable. Few non-professionals understand the nature of estate planning, and how assets will pass in the absence of a will. In addition, an attorney should be consulted so that she can appraise the situation and see if any estate tax planning is necessary as well. What the client doesn't know can always come back to bite her or her heirs.

Estate Taxation

Generally speaking, whatever an individual owns or has an interest in at the time of her death is subject to the federal estate tax. Both federal and state estate taxes must be paid within nine months of the date of death. For the year 2010, estates will be entirely free from federal taxation. However, the law that includes this provision expires at the end of 2010. Thus, unless Congress acts in the interim, in 2011 the estate tax rules will revert to those prevailing in 2002.

For 2008, the tax rate on estates is 45 percent as illustrated here:

Tax Year	Tax Rate	Exemption Equivalent
2007	45%	$2,000,000
2008	45%	$2,000,000
2009	45%	$3,500,000
2010	N/A	N/A
2011 and beyond	41-50%	$1,000,000

Not all estates, however, will be taxed while the estate tax is in effect. First, individuals can leave any amount of property to their spouses—if the surviving spouses are U.S. citizens—free of federal estate tax. This is due to the unlimited marital deduction. Second, due to an available credit, the estate tax essentially applies only to estates valued at more than $2 million in 2008 and this threshold will increase incrementally until it reaches $3.5 million in 2009 (see box). The federal government allows this tax credit for gifts made during an individual's life or for her estate upon her death. Third, gifts to charities are not taxed.

Most states also have an estate or inheritance tax. One simple way clients can reduce estate taxes or shelter assets in order to achieve Medicaid eligibility is to give some or all of their estate to their children (or anyone else) during their lifetimes in the form of gifts. Certain rules apply, however. There is a limit of $1 million on how much an individual may give tax free during her lifetime, but there is an exclusion for any gifts of up to $12,000. An individual may make gifts of up to $12,000 per recipient per year to an unlimited number of people. For any gift in excess of $12,000 (in 2007), a gift tax return reporting the gift to the IRS, must be filed. In addition, the amount above $12,000 will be counted against the $1 million lifetime tax exclusion for gifts. Each dollar of gift above $1 million reduces the amount that can be transferred tax-free in an individual's estate.

In addition, if a client is married, her spouse can duplicate these gifts. For example, a married couple with four children can give away up to $96,000 in 2008 with no gift tax implications. In addition, the gifts will not count as taxable income to their children (although the earnings on the gifts if they are invested will be taxed). For more on gifting, see the "Gifts to Grandchildren" section in this chapter.

Estate Administration

The emotional trauma brought on by the death of a close family member often is accompanied by bewilderment about the financial and legal steps the survivors must take. The spouse who passed away may have handled all of the couple's finances. Or perhaps a child must begin taking care of probating an estate about which she knows little. And this task may come in addition to other commitments to family and work that cannot be set aside. Finally, the estate itself may be in disarray or scattered among many accounts, which is not unusual with a generation that saw banks collapse during the Depression.

The following are various steps that the surviving family members should take upon the death of a loved one. These responsibilities ultimately fall on whoever is appointed executor or personal representative in the decedent's will. Matters can be a bit more complicated in the absence of a will, because it may not be clear who bears the responsibility of carrying out these steps.

First, the executor secures the decedent's tangible personal property. This means any physical material, such as jewelry, silverware, dishes, furniture, or artwork. The executor or personal representative will need to determine accurate values of each piece of property, which may require appraisals, and then later distribute the property as the decedent directed. If property is passed around to family members before the executor has had the opportunity to take an inventory, this will become a difficult, if not impossible, task. Of course, this does not apply to gifts the decedent may have made during life, which will not be part of her estate.

When the client is ready, advise her to meet with an attorney to review the steps necessary to administer the decedent's estate. Recommend she bring as much information as possible about the decedent's finances, taxes, and debts. The attorney handling the estate administration will have experience in organizing and understanding confusing financial statements.

The exact rules of estate administration differ from state to state. In general, they include the following steps:

1. Filing the will and petition at the probate court in order to be appointed executor or personal representative. In the absence of a will, heirs must petition the court to be appointed administrator of the estate.
2. Marshaling, or collecting, the assets. This means investigating everything the deceased owned during her lifetime. It is generally best to consolidate all the estate funds to the extent possible. Bills and bequests should be paid from a single checking account, so that the client can keep track of all expenditures.
3. Paying bills and taxes. If an estate tax return is needed, it must be filed within nine months of the date of death. If your client should miss this deadline and an estate tax is due, severe penalties and interest may apply. If the executor does not have all the information available in time, she can file for an extension and pay her best estimate of the tax due.
4. Filing tax returns. Your client must also file a final income tax return for the decedent and, if the estate holds any assets and earns interest or dividends, a fiduciary income tax return for the estate. In order to open up a bank account and file returns, the executor of the estate will have to obtain a tax identification number for the estate.
5. Distributing property to the heirs and legatees. Generally, executors do not pay out all of the estate assets until the period runs out for creditors to make claims, which can be as long as a year after the

date of death. But once the executor understands the estate and the likely claims, she can distribute most of the assets, retaining a reserve for unanticipated claims and the costs of closing out the estate. Prior to making distributions, the executor or administrator of the estate should obtain receipt and releases from each beneficiary.

6. Filing a final account. The executor must file an account with the probate court listing all of the estate assets as well as any income earned by the estate since the date of death as well as all expenses and estate distributions. In the case of a small estate or where close family members are the only ones involved, an informal accounting amongst the various involved parties might suffice. Once the court approves this final account, the executor can distribute whatever is left in the closing reserve, and finish her work.

Some of these steps can be eliminated by avoiding probate through joint ownership or trusts. But whoever is left in charge still has to pay all debts, file tax returns, and distribute the property to the rightful heirs. Recommend to your clients that they can make it easier for their heirs by keeping good records of their assets and liabilities. This will shorten the process and reduce the legal bill.

H.E.L.P. Healthcare and Elder Law Programs Corporation, a non-profit organization started by a California elder law attorney, offers a checklist to help survivors sort out and keep track of the things that need to be handled after a person has died. For more information, please visit http://www.better-endings.org/ and find the links to "When a Person Dies."

Wills

A will is a legally binding statement directing who will receive one's property upon death. It also appoints a legal representative, called an *executor*, *executrix*, or *personal representative*, to carry out the wishes of the person creating the will—the *testator* or *testatrix*. However, the will covers only probate property. Many types of property or forms of ownership pass outside of probate. Jointly-owned property, property in trust, life insurance proceeds, and property with a named beneficiary, such as IRAs or 401(k) plans, all pass outside of probate.

Why have a will? Here are some reasons:

First, a will can direct where and to whom an estate (assets held at death) will be distributed. If the testator dies intestate (without a will), her estate will be distributed according to her state's law. Such distribution may or may not accord with her wishes.

Many people try to avoid probate and the need for a will by holding all of their property jointly with their children. This can work, but often people spend unnecessary effort trying to make sure all the joint accounts remain equally distributed among their children. These efforts can be defeated by a long-term illness of the parent or the death of a child. A will can be a much simpler means of effectuating one's wishes about how assets should be distributed.

The second reason to have a will is to make administration of an estate run smoothly. Often the probate process can be completed more quickly and at less expense if there is a will. With a clear expression of a client's wishes, there are unlikely to be any costly, time-consuming disputes over who gets what.

Third, only with a will can a client choose the person to administer her estate and distribute it according to her instructions. This person is called an "executor" (or "executrix" if you appoint a woman) or "personal representative," depending on her state's statute. If she does not have a will naming a personal representative, the court will make the choice for her. Usually the court appoints the first person to ask for the post, whoever that may be, unless an heir objects, in which case the family is in for a lengthy, expensive, and bitter battle in court.

Fourth, for larger estates, a good estate plan that includes a properly drafted will can help reduce estate taxes.

Fifth, and most important, through a will a client can appoint a guardian of her minor children should both she and the other parent pass away.

Filling out a worksheet will help a client make decisions about what to put in her will. (For an ElderLawAnswers' Will Worksheet, refer to the companion CD-ROM of this book).

Trusts

A trust is a legal arrangement through which one person (or an institution, such as a bank or law firm), called a *trustee*, holds legal title to property for another person, called a *beneficiary*. The individual who contributes assets to the trust is referred to as the *grantor*. The rules or instructions under which the trustee operates are set out in the trust instrument. Trusts sometimes have one set of beneficiaries during the grantor's lifetime and another set—often the grantor's children—who begin to benefit only after the grantor has died. The first are often called *life beneficiaries* and the second *remaindermen*.

There can be several advantages to establishing a trust, depending on an individual's particular situation. One of the best-known benefits is the advantage of avoiding probate. In a trust that terminates with the death of the donor, any property in the trust prior to the donor's death passes immediately to the beneficiaries pursuant to the terms of the trust without requiring probate. This can save time and money for the beneficiaries. Certain trusts can also result in tax advantages both for the donor and the beneficiary. These are often referred to as *credit shelter* or *life insurance trusts*. A credit shelter trust, however, can also be created in someone's last will and testament. Other trusts may be used to protect property from creditors or to help the donor qualify for Medicaid. Unlike wills, trusts are private documents and only those individuals with a direct interest in the trust are privy to information regarding the trust assets and distributions. Provided they are well-drafted, another advantage of trusts is their continuing effectiveness even if the donor dies or becomes incapacitated.

Trustee Duties

The trustee of a trust is similar to the executor of a will. The grantor has granted her the fiduciary power to act on behalf of the trust and to carry out the terms of the trust. If an individual has been appointed as the trustee of a trust, this is a strong vote of confidence in her judgment and probity. Unfortunately, it is also a major responsibility.

In short, acting as trustee gives your client a wonderful opportunity to provide a great service to the trust's beneficiaries. The work can be very gratifying. A trustee must be prudent and constantly aware of the responsibilities described below in order to make sure that everything is in order so no one has grounds to question her actions at a later date.

Fiduciary Responsibility

As a trustee, your client stands in a *fiduciary* role with respect to the beneficiaries of the trust—both the current beneficiaries and any remaindermen named to receive trust assets upon the death of the grantor. As a fiduciary, the trustee is held to a very high standard, meaning that she must pay even more attention to the trust investments and disbursements than she would for her own accounts.

The Trust's Terms

Individuals and their advisors should read the trust document itself carefully, both at the time of the trust preparation and later, when any questions arise. The trust is your client's road map and she must follow its directions, whether about when and how to distribute income and principal or what reports she'll need to make to beneficiaries.

Investment Standards

A trustee's investments on behalf of the trust must be prudent, meaning that she cannot place money in speculative or risky investments. In addition, her investments must take into account the interests of both current and future beneficiaries. For instance, she may have a current beneficiary who is entitled to income from the trust. The beneficiary would be best off in most cases if the trust funds were invested in order to generate as much income as possible. However, this may be detrimental to the interest of later beneficiaries who would be happiest if the trustee invested for growth. In addition to balancing the interests of the various beneficiaries, the trustee must consider the beneficiaries' future financial needs. Does a trust beneficiary anticipate buying a house or going to school? Will the beneficiary be depending on the trust income for retirement in 15 years? All of these questions need to be considered in determining an investment plan for the trust. Only then can a trustee start considering the propriety of individual investments.

Distributions

If a trustee has discretion on whether or not to make distributions to a beneficiary, she must evaluate the beneficiary's current needs, her future needs, her other sources of income, and finally, the trustee's responsibilities to other beneficiaries before making a decision. And all of these considerations must be made in light of the size of the trust. Often the most important role of a trustee is the ability to say "no" and set limits on the use of the trust assets. This can be difficult when the need for current assistance is readily apparent.

Accounting

One of the jobs of the trustee is to keep track of all income to, distributions from, and expenditures by the trust. Generally, the trustee must give an account of this information to the beneficiaries on an annual basis, though she will need to check the terms of the trust to be sure. In strict trust accounting, the trustee must keep track of and report on principal and income separately.

Taxes

Depending on whether the trust is revocable or irrevocable and whether it is considered a *grantor* trust for tax purposes, the trustee will have to file an annual tax return and may have to pay taxes. In many cases, the trust will act as a pass through entity with the income being taxed to the beneficiary. In any event, if the trustee keeps good records and then turns the information over to the CPA to prepare, this should not pose a big problem.

Delegation

While a trustee cannot delegate her responsibilities as trustee, she can delegate all of the functions described above to you, the CPA. She can hire financial advisors to make investments, accountants to handle taxes and bookkeeping for the trust, and lawyers to advise her on questions of interpretation of the trust agreement. With such professional assistance, her job as trustee need not be difficult. However, she still needs to communicate with those she hires and make any discretionary decisions, such as when to make distributions of principal from the trust to one or more beneficiaries.

Fees

Trustees are entitled to reasonable fees for their services. Family members often do not accept fees, though that can depend on the work involved in a particular case, the relationship of the family member, and whether the family member trustee has been chosen due to her professional expertise. Determining what is reasonable can be difficult. Banks, trust companies, and law firms typically charge a percentage of the funds under management. Others may charge for their time. In general, what's reasonable depends on the work involved, the amount of funds in the trust, other expenses paid out by the trust, the professional experience of the trustee, and the overall expenses for administering the trust. For example, if the trustee has hired an outside firm for investment purposes, that might justify the trustee being paid a lower fee.

Testamentary and Inter Vivos Trusts

Trusts may be either *testamentary* or *inter vivos*.

A testamentary trust is one created by an individual's last will and testament, and it does not come into existence until the individual dies. Such a trust has no power or effect until the will of the decedent is probated. Although a testamentary trust will not avoid the need for probate and will become a public document as it is a part of the will, it can be useful in accomplishing other estate planning goals. For example, the testamentary trust can be used to reduce estate taxes upon the death of a spouse or provide for the care of a disabled child.

In contrast, an *inter vivos* trust starts during the individual's lifetime. The grantor creates the trust while she is alive and the trust is funded during her lifetime.

There are two kinds of *inter vivos* trusts: *revocable* and *irrevocable*.

Revocable Trusts

Revocable trusts are often referred to as *living* trusts. With a revocable trust, the grantor maintains complete control over the trust and may amend, revoke, or terminate the trust at any time. This means that the grantor can take back the funds she transferred to the trust or change the trust's terms. Thus, the grantor is able to reap the benefits of the trust arrangement while maintaining the ability to change the terms of the trust at any time prior to death. The trust, in essence, is an extension of the grantor.

Revocable trusts are generally used for the following purposes:

- **Asset management.** They permit the named trustee to administer and invest the trust property for the benefit of one or more beneficiaries.
- **Probate avoidance.** Upon the death of the person who created the trust, the trust property passes to whoever is named as a beneficiary in the trust. The trust agreement does not come under the jurisdiction of the surrogate or probate court and the distribution of the trust estate need not be held up by the probate process. However, the property of a revocable trust will be included in the grantor's estate for tax purposes.
- **Tax planning.** While the assets of a revocable trust will be included in the grantor's taxable estate, the trust can be drafted so that the assets will not be included in the estates of the beneficiaries, thus avoiding taxes when the beneficiaries die.

Irrevocable Trusts

An irrevocable trust cannot be changed or amended by the grantor. Any property placed into the trust may only be distributed by the trustee as provided for in the trust document itself. For example, the grantor may set up a trust under which she will receive income earned on the trust property, but will not have access to the trust principal. This type of irrevocable trust is a popular tool for Medicaid planning.

Supplemental Needs Trusts

The purpose of a supplemental needs trust is to enable the grantor to provide for the continuing care of a disabled spouse, child, relative, or friend. The beneficiary of a well-drafted supplemental needs trust will have access to the trust assets for purposes other than those provided by public benefits programs. In this way, the beneficiary will not lose eligibility for governmental benefits such as Supplemental Security Income, Medicaid, and low-income housing. A supplemental needs trust can be created by the donor during life or be part of a will.

Credit Shelter Trusts

A credit shelter trust is a vehicle through which one can take full advantage of the estate tax exemption. For the year 2008, the first $2 million of an estate will pass free of federal estate taxes. In theory, a husband and wife would have no federal estate tax if their combined estate is less than or equal to $4 million. However, if one spouse dies and leaves everything to the surviving spouse, the surviving spouse may have an estate that is greater than $2 million. Then, when the surviving spouse dies, any part of the estate over $2 million will be subject to estate tax. By leaving all of her assets to him, the first spouse to die effectively did not take advantage of her individual $2 million exemption.

To avoid this problem, the spouses can create credit shelter trusts as part of their estate plan. When the first spouse dies, the first $2 million of that spouse's estate will pass to a credit shelter trust rather than being paid directly to the surviving spouse. The surviving spouse may receive income from the trust, and together with an independent trustee can even dip into principal for his health, education, maintenance, or welfare, but as long as the he does not control the principal, the money will not be included in his estate when he passes away.

Alaska and Delaware Trusts

Special trusts set up in Alaska and Delaware can allow the grantor or donor of a trust to "have her cake and eat it, too." Such trusts can shield property from certain creditors while allowing the donor to still retain a benefit from the trust.

Traditionally, if the donor of a trust retains a benefit—such as access to some or all of the trust's property—creditors can collect from the trust up to the limit of that benefit. Some high-net-worth individuals have created trusts in other countries, known as *offshore* trusts, in order to be shielded from creditors and still reap a benefit from the trust.

In 1997, both Alaska and Delaware enacted laws to permit the creation of such trusts in their states (Nevada, Rhode Island, South Dakota, and Utah also have similar laws). So far, these trusts have been untested in court, but at least the statutes in these two states are clear. It is necessary in employing these trust forms to keep all assets invested in Alaska or Delaware institutions so that it falls to courts in these states to uphold the new statutes. The Alaska and Delaware trusts have the advantage over offshore arrangements of being less expensive to set up and maintain. In addition, many individuals may feel more comfortable having funds invested within the United States.

However, clients should be made aware that neither Alaska nor Delaware trusts are available to protect assets from already existing creditors or if the grantor or donor is in default of child support payments. The trust may not require that income or principal be distributed to the donor; such distributions must be discretionary. The donor also may not retain the right to revoke or amend the trust. In addition, Alaska requires that at least one trustee be a resident of Alaska and that at least $10,000 be maintained in an Alaskan bank or brokerage account. Alaska and Delaware trusts may also provide estate tax benefits. Normally, a taxpayer may not remove property from her estate while retaining any potential benefit (such as making a gift of money that the person making the gift still controls). But the IRS has stated that this combination is possible with these new trusts since creditors may not make any claim on the property.

Grandchildren

The relationship between a grandparent and a grandchild can be one of great joy and importance for both the grandparent and grandchild. Your clients may want to ensure the financial security of their grandchildren and there are several ways to do so, including gifts, gift trusts, and 529 accounts.

Sometimes an event such as a parent's death, divorce, or estrangement can tear families apart and alter or sever relationships. After such events, the child's parents or guardian may block any further contact with the child's grandparents, who may take legal steps to maintain contact with the grandchildren they love.

In this section, we will discuss some gifting options grandparents can make on behalf of their grandchildren, and we will also discuss an individual's rights when it comes to grandparent visitation.

Gifts to Grandchildren

Gifting assets to grandchildren can do more than help descendants get a good start in life; it can also reduce the size of an estate and the tax that will be due upon death.

Perhaps the simplest approach to gifting is to give the grandchild an outright gift. A client may give each grandchild up to $12,000 a year (in 2008) without having to report the gifts or be subject to any gift taxation. If your client is married, both she and her spouse can make such gifts. For example, a married couple with four grandchildren may give away up to $96,000 a year with no gift tax implications. In addition, the gifts will not count as taxable income to the grandchildren (although the earnings on the gifts if they are invested will be taxed).

However, some individuals may have misgivings about making outright gifts to their grandchildren. There is no guarantee that the money will be used in the way that they wish. Money that your client hoped would be saved for educational expenses may instead be spent on a vacation to Fort Lauderdale. Fortunately, there are a number of options to protect against misuse of the funds for grandchildren, such as direct payments to schools and custodial accounts.

Direct Payment for School or Health Costs

An individual can pay an unlimited amount for educational and medical costs for her grandchildren. Unlimited means that she can pay these expenses in addition to making annual $12,000 (in 2008) gifts without any gift tax consequences. The individual must be sure to pay the school or medical provider directly.

UGMA and UTMA

The Custodial Accounts Under the Uniform Gifts to Minors Act (UGMA) and the Uniform Transfers to Minors Act (UTMA) allow your client to make gifts to a custodial account that grandparents can establish for a minor grandchild. Since the account is in the name of the child, the tax liability is often shifted to the child, who presumably is in a lower tax bracket than your client or the grandchild's parents. Gifts to such accounts are irrevocable, but your client retains control of the money and decides how it will be invested.

UGMA and UTMA differ in the type of property they permit a person to transfer: States usually restrict UGMA investments to life insurance, cash, and certificates of deposit, while UTMA allows a wider variety of investments, including mutual funds, stocks, bonds, real estate, and even artwork.

Either type of account should be managed by someone other than the parent of the grandchild; otherwise, the parent will be responsible for taxes on the account income. For tax years starting in 2008, before a child reaches age 18, and if the child's income exceeds one-half of their support, the next $900 in income is taxed at the child's rate. Earnings above $1,800 are taxed at the parent's marginal rate.

The major downside of these accounts is that custodians must turn the money over to the child when she reaches the age of majority (18 or 21, depending on the state). The child may then do as she wishes with the money—and it may not be what your client would prefer. In addition, as with custodial accounts, the child's sudden ownership of the account funds could jeopardize her eligibility for financial aid for college. Visit http://www.finaid.org for more information.

Gift Trusts

Some gift options have serious drawbacks: there are no tax or estate planning advantages, your client has no control over the funds (or loses control after a certain point), or the money could affect, for instance, a grandchild's eligibility for financial aid. An option that overcomes many of these problems involves transferring money into a trust established for the benefit of a grandchild. With the help of an attorney, your client can draft a trust that reflects her express wishes about when the income and principal will be available to the grandchild and even how the funds will be spent.

Transferring funds into such a trust offers the following benefits:

- The size of an estate can be reduced, if an individual transfers up to $12,000 (in 2008) into each trust she creates for each grandchild. No gift taxes will be due in connection with the transfers.
- Although the trust owns the assets, the individual can control them as trustee and can decide what type of investments to make.
- Income earned by the trust from amounts that have been deposited will not be taxed to her; the trust pays the taxes.
- Amounts deposited in trust, and the income earned from those funds, will be used for the benefit of the individual's grandchildren.
- The individual can provide that the trust terminates at any age she specifies.

In order to qualify for these benefits, however, certain restrictions apply. These trusts are governed by complex legal documents and should not be set up without the help of an experienced attorney. As a result, the chief downside of such trusts is the cost of establishing and maintaining them, which your client should discuss with an attorney before moving forward.

As a final note on establishing such trusts, a client must be totally comfortable with this gift planning strategy and the amount of money available to her in her estate. In short, your client should only make gifts if she feels certain that the amount of funds remaining in her name and the amount of income they will produce will be adequate for her needs.

529 Accounts

This type of account, named for Section 529 of the Internal Revenue Code, enables an individual to reduce her taxable estate while earmarking funds for the higher education of a grandchild (or any other family member). Funds contributed to such accounts are invested to pay for a grandchild's college tuition, room and board, or other expenses. The account funds are usually invested in mutual funds, and the earnings from these accounts are tax-free.

Your client can contribute up to $12,000 (in 2008) per year ($24,000 for a couple) to 529 accounts without incurring a gift tax. Or, if she prefers, she can contribute up to $60,000 ($120,000 for a married couple) in the first year of a five-year period, as long as there are no additional gifts to that same beneficiary during the five years. In other words, 529 accounts can be a quick way of getting a sizable amount of money out of your client's taxable estate (although if she dies within the five-year period, the portion of the contribution allocated to the years following her death would be included in her estate). An added benefit is that donors to these accounts can take the money back later if needed, although they pay a penalty of 10 percent of earnings. (However, this power to control the assets means that the savings in a 529 account will be counted as an available asset under Medicaid rules in the event the account holder requires long-term care.)

If the grandchild uses the funds for any purpose other than higher education, the earnings are taxed as ordinary income to the account owner (your client), and a 10 percent penalty is assessed on investment gains. Since your client is the account owner, such accounts generally do not affect a grandchild's eligibility for financial aid. This change may increase a student's chances for financial aid since qualified withdrawals will no longer be considered income to the student. Moreover, your client can change beneficiaries at any time, as long as the new beneficiary is a member of the original beneficiary's family. Most states now permit or are planning to permit 529 account plans, and many investment firms now offer such plans as tax- and estate-planning vehicles for their clients.

The Web site www.savingforcollege.com can help your client compare the many state plans.

Other Gift Vehicles

The following sections contain information about other ways that individuals can make funds available to grandchildren and other beneficiaries.

IRAs

Clients can make contributions to their grandchildren's regular, Roth, or Educational IRAs.

Roth IRAs can be a particularly good way to help a grandchild build a nest egg. The amounts contributed to such accounts are not tax deductible, but the earnings accumulated can be withdrawn at age $59\frac{1}{2}$ completely tax-free (as long as certain conditions are met). This tax-free compounding can quickly add up: If a 15-year-old contributes $2,000 to a Roth today, the investment will be worth $146,000 when the child turns 60 (assuming a 10 percent annual return). Also, starting five years after the account has been set up, first-time home buyers can withdraw up to $10,000 tax-free. Furthermore, if Roth IRAs are used to pay college tuition, the earnings are taxed at the child's rate and early withdrawal penalties do not apply.

Savings Bonds

Don't overlook U.S. Savings Bonds, the most widely held type of security in the world. Bonds increase in value monthly and interest is compounded semiannually. Moreover, interest is free from state and local taxes, and federal income tax is deferred until your client redeems the bonds. Provided she meets certain eligibility requirements, you can reap special tax benefits if bonds are redeemed to pay for college expenses.

Series EE and the new Series I Bonds make great gifts for grandchildren. Series EE Bonds sell for half their face value. The bond denominations range from $50 to $10,000. If not redeemed when they mature, the bonds will continue to earn interest for up to 30 years. Series I (or Inflation-indexed) Savings Bonds come in denominations ranging from $50 to $10,000 and are issued at face value. The earnings rate, adjusted semiannually, is a combination of a fixed interest rate at the time of purchase and the rate of inflation. These bonds have a 30-year life. Current rates for both the EE and I Bond are available by calling 1-800-4USBond. Additional information on U.S. Savings Bonds can be found at the Web site www.savingsbonds.gov. Also, savings bonds can now be ordered directly on-line with a credit card!

More Options for Giving to Family

If your client has a taxable estate, other options may also exist, such as the creation of life insurance trusts and family limited partnerships. Check with an elder law attorney or tax advisor for more information about these planning options.

Reverse Mortgages[1]

3

People are living longer and experiencing financial strains as a result. Seniors can avoid economic hardship by taking advantage of a reverse mortgage. Specifically, financial hardships due to illness and long-term care issues, along with misinformation about the Medicare and Medicaid programs, place many seniors in a precarious financial position. The reverse mortgage was created to address the financial devastation experienced by seniors who are on fixed incomes and facing ever increasing housing, health, and living expense costs.

Under our system of paying for long-term care, older individuals may be able to qualify for Medicaid to pay for nursing home care. However, in most states there is little public assistance for home care. Most people want to remain at home as long as possible, but few can afford the high cost of home care for a lengthy period of time. One solution is for an individual to tap into built-up home equity by utilizing a reverse mortgage.

Reverse mortgages are somewhat underutilized now. But financial institutions, sensing an opportunity as the population ages and people live longer, are expanding their reverse mortgage programs. Although the market penetration is at about 1 percent, 89 percent of all reverse mortgages closed since 1989 (FHA/HECM) have been originated since 2000. Close to 350,000 such loans have originated through September of 2007 (Housing and Urban Development [HUD]'s fiscal year begins October 1st).

The topics that we will discuss in this chapter include the following:

- Introduction to reverse mortgages
- Is a reverse mortgage right for your client?

---

[1] Contributing author: Dennis Haber of Senior Funding Group, 247 West Old Country Road, Hicksville, NY 11801; Telephone: 1-516-570-5400 x208; Cell: 1-516-551-2189; E-mail: denhaber@aol.com.

Introduction to Reverse Mortgages

It is estimated that homes owned by seniors are worth $4.3 trillion and represent over $2 trillion that can be converted into cash. A 2007 press release by the National Reverse Mortgage Lenders Association (NRMLA) indicated that seniors, after having paid off their original mortgage or having significantly paid down the balance, prefer to have a mortgage that does not require monthly mortgage payments. According to HUD, the numbers of loans insured in their last two fiscal years (2006 and 2007), were 76,351 and 107,558, respectively. This represents more than half of all HECM reverse mortgages performed since the first one closed in 1989. Selling the home is not a desirable option for most seniors. They have lived in their homes for many years and find comfort in the familiar. By utilizing a reverse mortgage, the senior's home can provide a source of funds to maintain his life with the utmost dignity.

If an individual owns a home, uses it as his primary residence, and is at least 62 years old, he may be able to quickly get money to pay for long-term care (or anything else) by taking out a reverse mortgage. Reverse mortgages—financial arrangements designed specifically for older homeowners—are a way of borrowing that transforms your client's equity in a home into liquid cash without necessitating your client to move or make regular loan repayments. Reverse mortgages permit house-rich but cash-poor elders to use their housing equity to, for example, pay for home care while they remain in the home. The loans do not have to be repaid until the last surviving borrower dies, sells the home, or permanently moves out.

A traditional mortgage requires that monthly payments be made to the lender. As those payments are made, the unpaid principal balance decreases (amortizes), while home equity continues to grow. With a reverse mortgage, the opposite occurs. No monthly mortgage payments are ever required, and therefore, the unpaid reverse mortgage balance continues to grow. This, in turn, reduces the equity in the home. There are no income, asset, or credit requirements, and there is no personal liability (non-recourse).

A reverse mortgage also allows seniors, who otherwise couldn't afford it, to at least consider obtaining a long-term insurance care policy (providing, of course, that they meet the health underwriting requirements. These requirements differ from insurer to insurer).

How the Reverse Mortgage Works

In a reverse mortgage arrangement, the homeowner receives a sum of money from the lender, usually a bank, based largely on the value of the house, the age of the borrower, and current interest rates. For example, a 70-year-old borrower with a $200,000 house in Westchester County, New York would be able to receive a maximum loan of $116,000 (based on the expected interest rate during the week [November 20th, 2007] that the inputs were made; see chart below, which was created using AARP's Reverse Mortgage Calculator located at www.rmaarp.com). The lower the interest rate and the older the borrower, the more your client can borrow. The largest amount of cash that may be available through the HECM reverse mortgage program for three home values in Westchester County is illustrated in Table 3.1.

Table 3.1: Cash Available through HECM Depending on Home Values in Westchester County, New York

	Value of Home		
	$200,000	*$300,000*	*$400,000*
Age of Borrower		*Amount of Loan*	
65	$106,759	$164,209	$200,281
70	116,000	177,950	216,848
75	125,529	192,079	233,866
80	135,777	207,227	252,091
85	145,789	221,939	269,754
90	155,224	235,674	286,188

The Code of Federal Regulations (CFR) Title 24 Section 206.33 indicates that the age of the younger borrower is used when there are two borrowers. It is important to remember that older borrowers can convert more of the equity into cash. For example, assuming the same housing value in the same community, a 75-year-old borrower can extract more equity than a 65-year-old borrower.

Homeowners can receive the money in one of three ways (or in any combination of the three):

1.   In a lump sum
2.   As a line of credit that can be drawn on at the borrower's option
3.   In a series of regular payments, called a reverse annuity mortgage

The most popular choice is the line of credit because it allows a borrower to decide when he needs the money and how much to borrow. Moreover, no interest is charged on the untapped balance of the loan. However, the funds placed in the "line of credit bucket" will grow by at least 50 basis points. It is important to note that these funds are not invested. Rather, the credit limit is merely increasing. This is similar to a credit card company increasing a credit limit when the cardholder makes timely payments.

Although it is often assumed that an elderly person would want to use the funds from a reverse mortgage loan for his health care needs, there are no restrictions—the funds can be used in any way. For example, the loan can be used to pay back taxes, for house repairs, or to retrofit a home to make it handicapped-accessible. Seniors have used the proceeds to make needed home repairs, pay off credit card debt, judgments, mortgages, and tax liens. Some have used the proceeds for home health care requirements. Others have purchased second homes or traveled to their favorite places. The money can even be used to provide for a grandchild's college education. Some have even purchased different types of insurance policies.

Borrowers who take out a reverse mortgage still own their home. What is owed to the lender—and usually paid by the borrower's estate— is the money ultimately received over the course of the loan, plus interest. In addition, the repayment amount cannot exceed the value of the borrower's home at the time the loan is repaid. As we discussed earlier, all borrowers must be at least 62 years of age to qualify for a reverse mortgage. Any prior lien on the property must be paid off with the proceeds from the reverse mortgage.

Reverse mortgage approval is not based upon a showing of specific income, asset, or typical credit worthiness. The HUD Handbook 4235.1 Revision No. 1 paragraphs 4-3 (A, B, and C) indicate that any delinquent federal debt must be brought current or paid before HUD will let a senior be eligible for the HECM Program. To ensure that a closing can take place, all unsatisfied judgments and liens must be paid at or before closing. A

Chapter 7 bankruptcy must be discharged. A Chapter 13 filing must be approved by the court before a senior can receive a reverse mortgage.

A reverse mortgage works because a senior receives a sum of money from a bank without having to make those dreaded monthly payments [24 CFR §206.27(8)]. As long as the home is used as a primary residence (24 CFR §206.27(2)(i), 24 CFR §206.27(2)(ii),24 CFR §206.3 and 24 CFR §206.39), the property taxes are paid [24 CFR §206.27(6)], the homeowner's insurance is paid [24 CFR §206.27(6)], and the property is kept in good repair [24 CFR §206.27(5)], the loan does not have to be repaid. When the last spouse or homeowner passes away [24 CFR §206.27(c)] or does not use the property as his primary residence [24 CFR §206.27(2)(i)], then the loan must be repaid. At this time, the home is put on the market. The home is sold by the senior or his estate when he no longer has a use for the home.

Although the qualification process is easy, a reverse mortgage applicant must attend or receive reverse mortgage counseling from an approved counseling entity, such as HUD, or from the AARP Foundation Network of Counselors, which now includes counselors from the National Foundation of Credit Counselors and Money Management International (24 CFR §206.41 Mortgagee Letter 2005-44), before the process can go forward. This is a good thing, as it provides the seniors with additional information as well as possible alternatives to their situation. It ensures that the seniors are making an informed decision. As a further protective measure, a lender cannot start the actual processing of the loan until the counseling has been completed. Mortgagee letter 2004-25 allows such things as appraisal, title, credit report, etc., to be ordered after the counseling has been completed and the borrower has confirmed his desire to obtain a reverse mortgage. More recently, Mortgagee letter 2006-25 later amended 2004-25 to allow the ordering of a preliminary title report prior to counseling. This gives the parties an opportunity to solve any title problems that could take considerable time to fix.

Changes/Legislation

Many people think of reverse mortgages simply as a way to help our elders pay their bills. It is much more than that. In a short time the program has evolved into a very potent economic and financial tool. The National Governors Association, Centers for Medicare and Medicaid Services

(CMS), and The National Council on Aging have come out in favor of this program. The government, for example, is looking at reverse mortgages as a way to halt rising Medicaid costs. The passage of the Deficit Reduction Act by Congress is a case in point. It specifically makes any one that owns a home with $500,000 in equity ineligible for Medicaid benefits unless they obtain a home equity loan or a reverse mortgage (states have the opportunity to raise the amount to $750,000).

The steady increase in closed reverse mortgage (HECM) loans has caused Congress to increase the number of reverse mortgages the government can insure. The passage of additional legislation will permit HUD to insure an unlimited number of such loans. The United States Code (USC) Chapter 12 Section 1715z20(g) explains that HUD is authorized to insure 150,000 reverse mortgages. The number of HECM reverse mortgages has steadily increased. This figure is now approaching over 350,000. The FHA Modernization Bill passed the senate on December 14, 2007, by a vote of 93 to 1. Although the legislation as it pertained to reverse mortgages was identical, the bill passed by the Senate and the House differed on other FHA provisions and, therefore, these differences must first be settled by conference committee. The bill provides for the removal of the HECM cap (the amount of loans HUD can insure), provides for a single national loan limit ($417,000), insures reverse mortgages on co-op units, and lowers the origination fee from 2 percent to 1.5 percent of the maximum claim amount and allows for home purchase transactions. The passage of this bill would mean that the reverse mortgage program is here to stay. In effect, it is finally being recognized as the important financial instrument that it is. The program isn't immune to needs for change or concerns, however. The program has evolved, improved, and changed.

Equity Sharing Option Eliminated

The first decisive change to the reverse mortgage program occurred in 2000 with the elimination of the equity sharing option. This option originally allowed the lender to receive a portion of the appreciation on the subject property during the time the reverse mortgage was in place—in addition to the accrued interest. As a result, the industry learned a very expensive lesson. This egregious practice significantly slowed the growth of the program. Sadly, many people still erroneously believe that this practice exists today.

Locked-In Rate

The next change occurred in September of 2003. Up until that time, a senior borrower applying for a reverse mortgage would not know until closing how much money would be available at closing. This created a great deal of uncertainty and angst, as the borrower never knew what to expect. Today, the borrower knows that he cannot receive less than the amount disclosed at application. (This presupposes that the assumed property value is an accurate reflection of the appraised value). In essence, the rate that helps determine how much your client can receive is locked in. However, should this rate change in your client's favor, it's possible that he could receive more than the amount disclosed at application. This rate lock protection was further changed in August of 2006 by increasing the duration of the rate lock to 120 days from the time the case number is obtained.

Lower Margin

From the inception of the reverse mortgage program through 2006, all reverse mortgage loans were adjustable. The monthly adjustable was the preferred choice over the yearly adjustable (particularly when the margin on the annual adjustable climbed to 3.1 percent).

The HECM 1.50, which used a margin of 150 basis points over the Content Maturity Treasury (CMT) rate, has been the standard since the HECM program was created. 2007 ushered in a monthly adjustable rate utilizing a lower margin (by 50 basis points). This program is now referred to as the HECM 100 (this margin is 100 basis points over the CMT rate). This resulted in providing significantly more money to a senior borrower. 2007 also saw the introduction of the fixed rate Federal Housing Administration (FHA)/Home Equity Conversion Mortgage (HECM) reverse mortgage and the proprietary fixed rate reverse mortgage.

Closing Costs

Closing costs are a concern to some borrowers. A few proprietary programs have zero closing costs when a borrower takes the entire proceeds in one lump sum. Besides this, there are moves on several fronts to lower the costs on the FHA/HECM loans. The FHA Modernization Bill and the

Expanding Homeownership Act of 2007 seek to make key changes to the FHA/HECM reverse mortgage: to lower both the origination fees and the upfront FHA mortgage insurance premium; to permit the FHA reverse mortgage program to include co-op apartments; to allow purchase transactions; and to increase the amount of the home value used in calculating benefit amounts and create a single national loan limit.

HUD has also agreed to the use of different indices in determining rates (Mortgagee Letter 2007-13). While this was a concession to the secondary markets that are more comfortable using the London Interbank Offered Rate (LIBOR) index, it should also have the salutary effect of lowering rates. This, in turn, will put more money into the pockets of your clients.

Types of Reverse Mortgages

There are several distinct types of reverse mortgage loan programs. The three most common are (1) the HECM, (2) Fannie Mae's Homekeeper Loan and (3) the private proprietary program. We'll discuss these here in more detail.

Home Equity Conversion Mortgage (HECM)

The most widely available reverse mortgage product is the HECM—the only reverse mortgage program insured by the FHA. Based on revised data from the NRMLA revised press release on December 15th 2005, this program accounts for greater than 90 percent of all reverse mortgage loans obtained. The FHA sets a ceiling on the amount of the value of the home that can be counted toward determining the benefit amount. The top loan limit is currently $362,790. Since the determination is made on a county-by-county basis, a borrower will be provided greater proceeds for a home located in a county that utilizes the top limit. The limits usually change every year and are just one of the factors that determine how much one can receive. Age and expected interest rate are the other factors. As of this writing, the HECM lending limits range from a low of $200,160 to a high of $362,790. While these numbers will change over time, the basics of the program will remain stable. The FHA Modernization Bill H.R. 1852 passed the House of Representatives on September 19, 2007, by a margin of 348-72. Among other things, it provides for a single national loan limit of $417,000. This limit will only apply to the FHA/HECM reverse mortgage. This bill replaces The Reverse Mortgage To Help America's Seniors Act, which also passed the House of Representatives. This legislation died in the senate.

Fannie Mae Homekeeper Loan

The first proprietary reverse mortgage program was created in 1996: the Fannie Mae Homekeeper Loan. This program is more conservative than the HECM although the Fannie Mae (FNMA) lending limit is now $417,000.

HECM (24 CFR §206.3) and Homekeeper reverse mortgages can only be made against a principal residence. FHA will make a loan against a 1–4 family unit, approved condo, and Planned Unit Developments (PUDs) [24 CFR §206.45; Mortgagee Letter 90-17 (I); Mortgagee Letter 96-15;24 CFR §206.51; 12 USC §1715z-20(d)(3)]. However, single family lending limits are used in 2–4 unit properties. Fannie Mae will only make loans against 1 unit properties, approved condos, and PUDs.

One type of reverse mortgage program recently became available for co-ops: private proprietary programs. Let's discuss those next.

Private Proprietary Programs

The third type of reverse mortgage program is a private proprietary program, the first of which was created in 2001. These programs are usually for high-valued homes, typically $500,000 and higher, and provide more money than the FHA program would at that higher value. Private proprietary programs have also been used for co-ops, irrevocable trusts, and second homes (on a case-by-case basis).

The private proprietary program for co-ops is done only in a few jurisdictions. The State of New York was chosen because New York, particularly New York City, has a high density of cooperative apartments. This means that *tenant shareholders* of cooperative apartments in other omitted jurisdictions cannot take advantage of the reverse mortgage programs. The good news as of this writing is that HUD is considering the use of the HECM program for co-ops, which will impact all 50 states.

Is a Reverse Mortgage Right for Your Client?

While reverse mortgages look like no-lose propositions on the surface, they have some significant downsides. First, the closing costs for these loans are higher than those for conventional mortgages. Closing costs generally range from 5 percent to 12 percent of the benefit amount, depending upon the age of the borrower and upon the reverse mortgage program. These costs, based upon the HECM program using the benefit amounts for a 62-year-old up to a 95-year-old with a maximum claim amount of $362,790, can be financed by the loan itself, but that reduces the money available to the client.

Second, a reverse mortgage must be repaid when the homeowner no longer occupies the home. Therefore, if the homeowner requires long-term nursing home care, the reverse mortgage would have to be paid off. And typically, the only way to satisfy the reverse mortgage loan would be to sell the home. In many states, this could go counter to a Medicaid plan that has been implemented by the elder law professional.

Also, bear in mind that if an individual's major objective is to safeguard an inheritance for his children, a reverse mortgage may not be a good idea. As soon as the elderly borrower (or the surviving borrower) dies, it will be necessary to sell the home. But if an individual has a pressing need for additional income, has no close heirs, or both, or if he does not intend to benefit his children or his children do not particularly want to inherit the house, a reverse mortgage can be a way to supplement income, perhaps without jeopardizing Medicaid eligibility.

Reverse mortgages are complex products and borrowers are advised to acquaint themselves with the different options available and then carefully compare competing loan offerings. The following resources are available to help get you and your client started in that process:

- One can learn the basics about reverse mortgages from AARP's reverse mortgage Web site. The site includes a calculator for estimating the loan for which a borrower would be eligible. Visit www.aarp.org/revmort and www.reversemortgage.org (NRMLA).
- For more details, background information, and supplementary materials, visit the National Center for Home Equity Conversion's site at www.reverse.org and NRMLA's site at www.reversemortgage.org.
- The names of FHA-insured lenders are available from the Federal National Mortgage Association (Fannie Mae), 1-800-7-FANNIE, and from NRMLA at www.reversemortgage.org.

Medicaid and Medicaid Planning

4

Medicaid is a joint federal-state program that provides health insurance coverage to low-income children, seniors, and people with disabilities. In addition, it covers care in a nursing home for those who qualify, as well as home care in some states. In the absence of any other public program covering long-term care, Medicaid has become the default nursing home insurance for the middle class.

As for home care, Medicaid offers very little coverage in most states except for New York, which provides home care on a more extensive basis to Medicaid recipients. Recognizing that home care typically costs far less than nursing home care, a few other states—notably Hawaii, Massachusetts, Oregon, and Wisconsin—are pioneering efforts to provide Medicaid-covered services to those who remain in their homes. New York State even provides for some Medicaid fund-assisted living care in its so-called Assisted Living Program facilities. The result of these community-based programs is that the individual can remain at home or in an assisted living facility for a longer period of time, thereby reducing the need and costs for nursing home care.

While Congress and the federal centers for Medicare and Medicaid services set out the main rules under which Medicaid operates, each state runs its own program. As a result, the rules are somewhat different in every state, although the basic framework is the same throughout the country.

You can help your clients plan for Medicaid using the information and advice we are providing in this chapter.

The topics that we will discuss in this chapter include the following:

- Medicaid
- Medicaid planning

Medicaid

For all practical purposes, the only viable insurance plan in the United States for long-term institutional care is Medicaid. Lacking access to alternative means of coverage, such as paying privately or being covered by a long-term care insurance policy, most people pay out of their own pockets for long-term care until they become eligible for Medicaid. Although their names are confusingly similar, Medicaid and Medicare are quite different programs. First, all retirees who receive Social Security benefits also receive Medicare as their health insurance. Medicare is an *entitlement* program and is not means tested. Medicaid, on the other hand, is only available for the indigent. Accordingly, in order to be eligible for Medicaid, one must be impoverished under the program's guidelines.

In addition, unlike Medicare, which is only based federally, Medicaid is a joint federal-state program. Each state operates its own Medicaid system, but this system must conform to federal guidelines in order for the state to receive federal funds that cover approximately half of the state's Medicaid costs. (The state picks up the rest of the tab. In some states, the local county picks up a small percentage of the Medicaid cost.)

This dual system complicates matters since the Medicaid eligibility rules are somewhat different from state to state, and they keep changing. (Some states also have their own names for the program, such as "MediCal" in California and "MassHealth" in Massachusetts.) Both the federal government and most state governments continually tinker with the eligibility requirements and restrictions. This most recently occurred with the passage of the Deficit Reduction Act of 2005 (DRA), signed by President Bush on February 8, 2006, which significantly changed the rules governing the treatment of asset transfers and homes of nursing home residents. (The DRA will be discussed in more detail later on in this section.) The implementation of these changes is proceeding on a state-by-state basis and will continue to do so over the course of the next few years. The following section covers the general Medicaid eligibility rules in accordance with federal guidelines. Specific rules, however, may differ from state to state.

Resource (Asset) Rules

In order to be eligible for Medicaid benefits, a nursing home resident may have no more than $2,000 in *countable* assets. This figure varies slightly from state-to-state. For example, in New York, the resource level is $4,350 for 2008.

The spouse of a nursing home resident, referred to as the *community spouse*, is limited to owning one half of the couple's joint assets up to a maximum of $104,400 (in 2008) in countable assets (see the section "Protections for the Healthy Spouse" later in this chapter). This figure changes each year to reflect inflation. In addition, the community spouse may keep the first $20,880 (in 2008), even if that is more than half of the couple's assets. This figure can be higher in some states (for example, the figure is $74,820 or 1/2 of the spouse's resources, but no greater than $104,400 in New York).

All assets are included against these limits unless the assets fall within the short list of *noncountable* assets. These include

- personal possessions, such as clothing, furniture, and jewelry;
- one motor vehicle, valued up to $4,500 for unmarried recipients or up to any value for the healthy community spouse;
- the applicant's principal residence, valued up to $500,000 in equity (or up to $750,000 at the state's option, provided it is in the same state in which the individual is applying for coverage [the states vary in whether the Medicaid applicant must prove a reasonable likelihood of being able to return home]);
- prepaid funeral plans and a small amount of life insurance;
- assets that are considered inaccessible for one reason or another; and
- retirement accounts such as IRAs are exempt resources in some states provided certain requirements are met.

With respect to the personal residence, nursing home residents, depending on the state, do not have to sell their homes in order to qualify for Medicaid. Under the DRA, principal residences may be deemed noncountable if their equity is less than $500,000, with the states having the option of raising this limit to $750,000. In some states, the home will not be considered a countable asset for Medicaid eligibility purposes as long as the nursing home resident intends to return home; in other states, the nursing home resident must prove a likelihood of returning home. In all states, the house may be kept with no equity limit if the Medicaid applicant's spouse or another dependent relative (that is, a minor under the age of 21, a blind, or a disabled child) lives there.

Transfers

Congress has established a period of ineligibility for Medicaid for those who transfer (that is, gift) assets. The DRA significantly changed rules governing the treatment of asset transfers. For transfers made prior to the enactment of the DRA on February 8, 2006, state Medicaid officials will look only at transfers made within the 36 months prior to the Medicaid application (or 60 months if the transfer was made to or from certain kinds of trusts). For transfers made after the passage of the DRA, the so-called *look-back period* for all transfers is 60 months.

The look-back period determines what transfers will be penalized, while the length of the penalty on the amount transferred is determined by dividing the amount transferred by the average monthly cost of nursing home care in the state. Some states, such as New York, calculate the average monthly cost of nursing home care by regions. For instance, if the nursing home resident transferred $100,000 in a state where the average monthly cost of care was $5,000, the penalty period would be 20 months (100,000 ÷ $5,000 = 20).

Another significant change in the treatment of transfers made by the DRA concerns the start of the penalty period created by the transfer. Under the prior law, the 20-month penalty period created by a transfer of $100,000 in the example described above would begin either on the first day of the month during which the transfer occurred or on the first day of the following month, depending on the state. Under the DRA, the 20-month period will not begin for a client until

- the transferor is receiving nursing home care;
- the client has spent or gifted assets down to the resource limit for Medicaid eligibility;
- the client has applied for Medicaid coverage; and
- the client is otherwise eligible for the Medicaid coverage but not for the transfer.

For example, if an individual transfers $100,000 on April 1, 2006, moves to a nursing home on April 1, 2007, and spends down to Medicaid eligibility on April 1, 2008, the 20-month penalty period will not begin until either April or May of 2008 (depending on the state), and it will not end until December 1, 2009. How this change is implemented from state-to-state will be determined over the course of the next few years.

Transfers of assets should be made carefully with an understanding of all the consequences. People who make transfers must not apply for Medicaid before the five-year look-back period elapses without first consulting with an elder law attorney. This is because the penalty could ultimately extend even longer than five years, depending on the size of the transfer.

One of the prime planning techniques used prior to the enactment of the DRA was for the Medicaid applicant to give away approximately half of her assets. Before applying for Medicaid, the prospective applicant would transfer half of her resources, thus creating a Medicaid penalty period. The applicant, who was often already in a nursing home, then used the other half of her resources to pay for her care while waiting out the ensuing penalty period. After the penalty period expired, the individual could apply for Medicaid coverage. This plan was often referred to as the "half a loaf" or "rule of halves" plan.

> **Example:** Mrs. Jones had savings equal to $72,000. The average private-pay nursing home rate in her state is $6,000 a month. When she entered a nursing home, she transferred $36,000 of her savings to her son. This created a six-month period of Medicaid ineligibility ($36,000 ÷ $6,000 = 6). During these six months, she used the remaining $36,000 plus her monthly income to pay privately for her nursing home care. After the six-month Medicaid penalty period had elapsed, Mrs. Jones would have spent down her remaining assets and be able to qualify for Medicaid coverage.

While a client could generally give away approximately half of her assets, the exact amount depended on a variety of factors, including the cost of care, the monthly regional rate in her state, her monthly income, and any other possible expenses. One of the main goals of the DRA was to eliminate this kind of planning. Elder law practitioners in all states have attempted to devise alternative planning to help preserve clients' assets. Among other techniques, such plans include the use of promissory notes and annuities. For example, in New York, it is currently commonplace to preserve approximately half of the applicant's assets at the eleventh hour through the use of gifting along with a promissory note drafted in accordance with DRA guidelines. The protected assets are typically used by the family to pay for extra care, such as an additional aide or attendant, for the recipient in the nursing home.

Any transfer strategy must take into account the applicant's income and all of her expenses, including the cost of the nursing home. In addition, one should bear in mind that if a client transfers assets to her children, it becomes their assets, subject to their individual whims and financial predicaments. However well-intentioned her children may be, they could lose the funds due to bankruptcy, divorce, or lawsuit. Any of these occurrences would jeopardize the savings a client spent a lifetime accumulating. Clients should be advised not to give away their savings unless they are ready to face these risks.

In addition, clients should be made aware of the fact that children holding funds in their names could jeopardize their children's eligibility for financial aid in college. Transfers can also have negative tax consequences. This is especially true of assets that have appreciated in value, such as real estate and stocks. If a client gives these assets directly to her children, the children will not get the tax advantages they would normally get if they were to receive such assets through their parent's estate. The result is that when the children sell the property, they will have to pay a much higher tax on capital gains than they would have if they had inherited it.

In light of the above, transfers should be made with great care and with an understanding of all the consequences. As a rule, individuals should never transfer assets for Medicaid planning unless they retain enough funds in their own name to (1) pay for any long-term health care needs they may have during the resulting period of ineligibility for Medicaid; and (2) they feel comfortable and have sufficient resources to maintain their present lifestyles.

Even though a nursing home resident may receive Medicaid benefits while owning a home (the DRA has restricted Medicaid eligibility for some homes), if she is married, she should transfer the home in full to the community spouse (assuming the nursing home resident is both willing and competent). As discussed below, any transfers of assets to a community spouse are exempt from Medicaid penalty periods. This gives the community spouse control over the asset and allows the community spouse to sell it after the spouse in the nursing home becomes eligible for Medicaid. In addition, the community spouse should change his will to bypass the nursing home spouse. Otherwise, if the community spouse pre-deceases the ill spouse, the home and other assets of the community spouse will pass to the nursing home spouse and will jeopardize her nursing home eligibility. It is important to note that some states have what is known as right of election laws that prohibit one spouse from totally dis-inheriting the other. The ramifications of these *right of election* laws regarding Medicaid eligibility vary from state to state.

Permitted Transfers

While most transfers are penalized with a period of Medicaid ineligibility of up to five years, certain transfers are exempt from this penalty. Even after entering a nursing home, an individual may transfer any asset to one of the following individuals without having to wait out a period of Medicaid ineligibility:

- A spouse
- A child who is blind or permanently disabled
- A trustee of a trust created for the sole benefit of anyone under age 65 and permanently disabled

In addition, an individual may transfer her home to one of the following individuals (as well as to those listed above):

- A child who is under age 21
- A child who has lived in her home for at least two years prior to her moving to a nursing home and who provided care that allowed her to stay at home during that time
- A sibling who already has an equity interest in the house and who lived there for at least one year before the individual moved to a nursing home

Treatment of Income

The basic Medicaid rule for nursing home residents is that they must pay all of their income, less certain deductions, to the nursing home. The deductions include a $60-a-month personal needs allowance (this amount may be somewhat higher or lower in particular states), a deduction for any uncovered medical costs (including medical insurance premiums), and, in the case of a married applicant, an allowance for the spouse who continues to live at home if she needs income support. A deduction may also be allowed for a dependent child living at home.

In some states, known as *income cap* states, eligibility for Medicaid benefits is barred if the nursing home resident's income exceeds $1,911 a month (for 2008), unless the excess above this amount is paid into a *(d)(4)(B)* or *Miller* trust. If an individual lives in an income cap state and requires more information on such trusts, she should consult an elder law attorney in the state in which she resides.

For married Medicaid applicants who have a spouse residing in the community, the income of the community spouse is not counted in determining the Medicaid applicant's eligibility. Only income in the applicant's name is counted in determining her eligibility. Thus, even if the community spouse is still working and earning $5,000 a month, he will not have to contribute to the cost of caring for his spouse in a nursing home if she is covered by Medicaid. (Some states, however, require that a portion of the community spouse's income, if over a certain amount, be applied to the cost of the ill spouse's care.)

Protections for the Healthy Spouse

The Medicaid law provides special protections for the spouse of a nursing home resident to make sure he has the minimum support needed to continue to live in the community.

These *spousal protections* work as follows: If the Medicaid applicant is married, the countable assets of both the community spouse and the institutionalized spouse are totaled as of the *date of institutionalization*, the day on which the ill spouse enters either a hospital or a long-term care facility in which she then stays for at least 30 days. (This is sometimes called the *snapshot date* because Medicaid is taking a picture of the couple's assets as of this date.)

In most states, the community spouse may keep one half of the *couple's* total countable assets up to a maximum of $104,400 (in 2008). This sum is called the *community spouse resource allowance* (CSRA) and is the most that a state may allow a community spouse to retain without a hearing or a court order. The least that a state may allow a community spouse to retain is $20,000 (in 2008), although many states have set a higher minimum CSRA.

> **Example:** If a couple has $100,000 in *countable* assets on the date the applicant enters a nursing home, the applicant will be eligible for Medicaid once the couple's assets have been reduced to a combined figure of $52,000—$2,000 for the applicant and $50,000 for the community spouse.

Some states, however, are more generous toward the community spouse. In these states, the community spouse may keep up to $104,400 (in 2008), regardless of whether or not this represents half the couple's assets.

> **Example:** If the couple had $60,000 in countable assets on the snapshot date, the community spouse could keep the entire amount instead of being limited to $30,000.

In all circumstances, Medicaid will not interfere with the allowable income of the community spouse; the community spouse will not have to use his income to support the nursing home spouse receiving Medicaid benefits. In a situation where most of the couple's income is in the name of the institutionalized spouse, and the community spouse's income is not enough to live on, the community spouse is entitled to some or all of the monthly income of the institutionalized spouse. How much the community spouse is entitled to depends on what the Medicaid agency determines to be the minimum income level for the community spouse. This figure, known as the minimum monthly maintenance needs allowance (MMMNA), is calculated for each community spouse according to a complicated formula. The MMMNA may range from a low of $1,711 (from July 1, 2007–June 30, 2008) to a high of $2,610 a month (for the end of 2008). (The low figure rises to $1,750 by July 1, 2008.) If the community spouse's own income falls below his MMMNA, the shortfall is made up from the nursing home spouse's income.

> **Example:** Mr. and Mrs. Smith have a joint income of $2,400 a month, $1,700 of which is in Mrs. Smith's name and $700 of which is in Mr. Smith's name. Mrs. Smith enters a nursing home and applies for Medicaid. The Medicaid agency determines that Mr. Smith's MMMNA is $1,700 (based on his housing costs). Since Mr. Smith's own income is only $700 a month, the Medicaid agency allocates $1,000 of Mrs. Smith's income to his support. As Mrs.

Smith also may keep a $60 a month personal needs allowance, her obligation to pay the nursing home is $640 a month ($1,700 – $1,000 – $60 = $640).

In exceptional circumstances, community spouses may seek an increase in their MMMNAs either by appealing to the state Medicaid agency or by obtaining a court order of spousal support.

Estate Recovery and Liens

Under Medicaid law, following the death of the Medicaid recipient, a state must attempt to recover from her estate whatever benefits it paid for the recipient's care. However, no recovery can take place until the death of the recipient's spouse, or as long as there is a child of the deceased who is under age 21, blind, or disabled.

While a state must attempt to recover funds from the Medicaid recipient's probate estate, meaning property that is held in the Medicaid recipient's name only (not in held a trust or with a beneficiary designation), a state has the option under federal law to seek recovery against property in which the recipient had an interest and which passes outside of probate. This includes jointly held assets, assets in a living trust, or life estates. Given the rules for Medicaid eligibility, the only probate property of substantial value that a Medicaid recipient is likely to own at death is her home. However, states that have not opted to broaden their estate recovery to include non-probate assets may not make a claim against the Medicaid recipient's home if it is not in her probate estate.

In addition to the right to recover from the estate of the Medicaid recipient, state Medicaid agencies must place a lien on real estate owned by the Medicaid recipient during her life unless certain dependent relatives are living on the property. If the property is sold while the Medicaid beneficiary is living, not only will she cease to be eligible for Medicaid due to the cash she would net from the sale, but she would have to satisfy the lien by paying back the state for its coverage of her care to date. The exceptions to this rule are cases where a spouse, a disabled or blind child, a child under age 21, or a sibling with an equity interest in the house is living in the property.

Whether or not a lien is placed on the house, the lien's effect should only be for recovery of Medicaid expenses if the house is sold during the beneficiary's life. The lien should be removed upon the beneficiary's death. However, this varies from state to state, and, therefore, it is imperative to check with an elder law attorney in your state to see how your local agency applies this federal rule.

The Treatment of Annuities

The DRA added requirements for disclosing immediate annuities, which have been useful long-term care planning tools. In its simplest form, an immediate annuity is a contract with an insurance company under which the consumer pays a certain amount of money to the company and the company then sends the consumer a monthly check for the rest of her life or for a prescribed time period.

An immediate annuity can be used to convert assets into an income stream for the benefit of an institutionalized Medicaid applicant or the community spouse. The state will not treat the annuity as an asset countable toward Medicaid's asset limit ($2,000 in most states plus up to $104,400 for the community spouse) as long as the annuity complies with certain requirements. The annuity must be

- **irrevocable.** The annuitant cannot take funds out of the annuity except for the monthly payments;
- **non-transferable.** The annuitant cannot be able to transfer the annuity to another beneficiary; and
- **actuarially sound.** The payment term cannot be longer than the annuitant's life expectancy and the total of the anticipated payments must equal the cost of the annuity.

The DRA added an additional requirement. In order for the annuity not to be treated as a countable asset, the state must be named the remainder beneficiary up to the amount of Medicaid benefits paid on the nursing home resident's behalf. If the Medicaid recipient is married or has a minor or disabled child, the state must be named as a secondary beneficiary. The Medicaid application must now also inform the applicant that if she obtains Medicaid benefits, the state automatically becomes a beneficiary of the annuity.

In addition, all annuities must be disclosed by an applicant for Medicaid regardless of whether the annuity is irrevocable or treated as a countable asset. If an individual, spouse, or representative refuses to disclose sufficient information related to any annuity, the state must either deny or terminate coverage for long-term care services or else deny or terminate Medicaid eligibility.

Promissory Notes and Life Estates

Prior to the DRA's enactment, in most states, a Medicaid applicant was able to prove that a transfer was really a loan to another person rather than a countable gift by presenting promissory notes, loans, or mortgages at the time of the Medicaid application. A promissory note is normally given in exchange for a loan, and it is simply a promise to repay the specified amount. Classifying transfers as loans rather than as gifts is useful because it allows parents to "loan" assets to their children and still maintain Medicaid eligibility.

Congress considered this to be an abusive planning strategy, so the DRA has imposed restrictions on the use of promissory notes, loans, and mortgages. In order for a loan to be treated as exempt from the transfer penalty rules, it must satisfy three standards: (1) the term of the loan must not last longer than the anticipated life of the lender; (2) payments must be made in equal amounts during the term of the loan with no deferral of payments and no balloon payments; and (3) the debt cannot be cancelled at the death of the lender. If these three standards are not met, the outstanding balance on the promissory note, loan, or mortgage will be considered a transfer and used to assess a Medicaid penalty period. If this strategy is to be successful, some states require that the loan, note, or mortgage be irrevocable and non-assignable.

Prior to the DRA's passage, another common estate planning technique was for an individual to purchase a life estate (a legal right to live in and possess a property) in the home of another person, such as a child. By doing this, the individual was able to pass assets to her children without triggering a transfer penalty because this was a purchase and not a gift. The DRA still allows the purchase of a life estate in another person's home, but to avoid a transfer penalty the individual purchasing the life estate must actually reside in the home for at least one year after the purchase.

Undue Hardship Exception

Before the DRA's passage, federal law allowed for an exemption from the transfer penalty if it would cause *undue hardship*, but the law did not establish procedures for determining undue hardship and left it up to states to create their own. The DRA finally sets out some rules and requires states to create a hardship waiver process that complies with specific language in the federal law. The new law provides that undue hardship exists if enforcing the penalty period for asset transfers would deprive the Medicaid applicant of (1) medical care necessary to maintain the applicant's health or life or (2) food, clothing, shelter, or necessities of life.

If an applicant asserts an undue hardship, state Medicaid agencies must approve or deny the application within a reasonable time, must inform the applicant that she has the right to appeal the decision if denied, and must provide a process by which this appeal can be made. In addition, the applicant must be told that application of the penalty period can be halted if undue hardship exists. Interestingly, with the resident's consent, nursing homes may now pursue hardship wavers on their behalf.

State Long-Term Care Partnerships

Many middle-income people have too many assets to qualify for Medicaid but cannot afford an expensive long-term care insurance policy. The DRA now permits all states to participate in so-called *partnership* programs, previously available in only four states—California, Connecticut, Indiana, and New York. Partnership long-term care insurance policies allow buyers to protect assets and qualify for Medicaid when the term of the long-term care policy runs out. In an effort to encourage more people to purchase long-term care insurance, the DRA allows all states to create such programs. For more on these programs, see Chapter 6, "Long-term Care Insurance," and specifically the section called "Partnership Policies."

Continuing Care Retirement Communities

The DRA now expressly allows continuing care retirement communities (CCRCs) to require residents to spend down their declared resources before applying for Medicaid. However, the spend-down requirements must still take into account the income needs of the Medicaid applicant's spouse. The DRA also requires that three conditions be met before a CCRC entrance fee can be considered an available resource of someone applying for Medicaid coverage of nursing home care. It must be allowable for the entrance fee to be used to pay for the individual's care, the fee or any remaining portion must be refundable upon the institutionalized individual's death or upon termination of the admission contract when the individual leaves the CCRC, and the fee must not grant the individual an ownership interest in the CCRC.

Medicaid Planning

One of the greatest fears of the elderly and disabled is that they may end up in a nursing home. This not only means a great loss of personal autonomy, but also a tremendous financial price. Depending on location and level of care, nursing homes cost between $35,000 and $150,000 a year.

Most people end up paying for nursing home care out of their savings until their money runs out. Then they can qualify for Medicaid to pick up the cost of care. In some states, there is an advantage to paying privately for nursing home care. In those states, private pay patients are more likely to gain entrance to a better quality facility, and paying privately eliminates or postpones dealing with the state's welfare bureaucracy, an often demeaning and time-consuming process. The disadvantage is that the cost is prohibitively expensive.

Careful planning, whether in advance or in response to an unanticipated need for care, can help protect a client's estate, whether for her spouse or for her children. This can be effected by purchasing long-term care insurance or by ensuring that the client is eligible to receive the benefits to which she is entitled under the Medicare and Medicaid programs. Veterans may also seek benefits from the Veterans Administration.

Those who are not in immediate need of long-term care may have the luxury of distributing or protecting their assets in advance. This way, when they do need long-term care, they will quickly qualify for Medicaid benefits. Setting forth general rules for so-called Medicaid planning is difficult because every client's case is different. Some have more savings or income than others. Some are married, others are single. Some have family support, others do not. Some own their own homes, some rent. Still, a number of basic strategies and tools are typically used in Medicaid planning, which will be discussed in this chapter. It is important to understand the limits and restrictions of Medicaid planning, but first, it is important to get a quick overview of the role that Medicare plays in all of this.

Medicare

Medicare Part A covers up to 100 days of skilled nursing care per spell of illness. However, the definition of "skilled nursing" and the other conditions for obtaining this coverage are quite stringent, meaning that few nursing home residents receive the full 100 days of coverage. As a result, Medicare pays for only about 9 percent of nursing home care in the United States. Please refer to Chapter 5, "Medicare," for tips on making sure a client receives the nursing care benefits to which she is entitled.

Trusts

In recalling the discussion of transfers from earlier in the chapter, the problem with transferring assets is that a client must relinquish complete control. She no longer has an ownership interest in the assets transferred, and even a trusted child or other relative may lose or deplete the gifted assets. A safer approach is to transfer the assets to a properly drafted irrevocable trust. A trust is a legal entity under which one person, the *trustee*, holds legal title to property for the benefit of others, that is, the *beneficiaries*. The trustee must follow the rules provided in the trust instrument. Whether trust assets are counted against Medicaid's resource limits depends on the terms of the trust and who created it.

A *revocable* trust is one that may be changed or rescinded by the person who created it. Medicaid considers the principal of such trusts (that is, the funds that make up the trust) to be assets that are countable in determining Medicaid eligibility. Thus, revocable trusts, although often utilized in an estate planning context, are of limited use in Medicaid planning.

Income-only Trusts

An *irrevocable* trust, on the other hand, is one that cannot be revoked or amended after it has been created. In most cases, this type of trust is drafted so that only the income is payable to the person establishing the trust, (that is, the *grantor*) for life, while the principal will not be available to or used for the benefit of the grantor or the grantor's spouse. The grantor is sometimes also referred to as the *settlor* or *trustor*. Upon the grantor's death, the principal is paid to the grantor's beneficiaries. This way, the funds in the trust are protected and the grantor can use the income for living expenses. For Medicaid purposes, the principal in such trusts is not counted as a resource, provided the trustee cannot pay it to the grantor or her spouse for their benefit. However, if the grantor does move to a nursing home, the trust income will have to be paid to the nursing home or budgeted to the community spouse with limited income.

A client should be aware of the drawbacks to such an arrangement. It is very rigid, so the client will not have access to the trust funds even if she needs them for some other purpose. For this reason, a client should always leave an ample cushion of readily available funds outside the trust.

A client, the grantor, may also choose to place property in a trust from which payments of income to her or her spouse cannot be made. Instead, the trust may be set up so that the income beneficiaries are the client's children or other third parties. These beneficiaries may, at their discretion, return the favor by using the property for your client's benefit, if necessary. However, there is no legal requirement that they do so.

One advantage of these trusts is that if they contain property that has increased in value, such as real estate or stock, the grantor can retain a *special testamentary power of appointment* so that the beneficiaries receive the property with a step-up in basis upon the grantor's death. This will also prevent the need to file a gift tax return upon the funding of the trust because transfers to such irrevocable trusts are deemed *incomplete gifts* for IRS purposes.

It is important to remember, however, that funding an irrevocable trust can cause a client to be ineligible for Medicaid nursing home coverage for up to five years after assets are transferred to the trust.

Testamentary Trusts

Testamentary trusts are trusts created under a will and do not go into effect until the testator—the person who wrote the will—dies. The Medicaid rules provide a special *safe harbor* for testamentary trusts created by a deceased spouse for the benefit of a surviving spouse. The assets of these trusts are treated as available to the Medicaid applicant only to the extent that the trustee has an obligation to pay for the applicant's support. If payments are solely at the trustee's discretion, they are considered unavailable.

Therefore, these testamentary trusts can provide an important mechanism for community spouses to leave funds that can be used to pay for services that are not covered by Medicaid for their surviving institutionalized spouses. These may include extra therapy, special equipment, evaluation by medical specialists or others, legal fees, visits by family members, or transfers to another nursing home if that should become necessary.

Supplemental Needs Trusts

The Medicaid rules also have certain exceptions for transfers to or for the sole benefit of disabled individuals under the age of 65. Even after admission to a nursing home, if an applicant has a disabled child, other disabled relative, or even a friend who is under age 65 and disabled, she can transfer assets into a trust for the disabled person's benefit without incurring any period of ineligibility. If these trusts are properly structured, the funds in them will not be considered to belong to the beneficiary in determining the beneficiary's own Medicaid eligibility. The only drawback to supplemental needs trusts (also called *special needs trusts*) is that after the disabled individual dies, the state must be reimbursed for any Medicaid funds spent on behalf of the disabled person.

Protection of the House

As we explained in the Medicaid section of this chapter, upon the death of a Medicaid recipient, the state must attempt to recoup from her probate estate whatever benefits it paid for her care. This is referred to as *estate recovery*.

Life Estate

For many people, transferring their home to their children subject to a *life estate* is the most simple and appropriate alternative for protecting their home from estate recovery. A life estate is the retention of the right to the possession, use, and control of the home during the transferor's lifetime. Both the transferor and the transferee have an ownership interest in the property, but for different periods of time. The person holding the life estate possesses the right to use the property currently and for the rest of her life. The transferee has a current ownership interest but cannot take possession until the end of the life estate, which occurs upon the death of the life estate holder. As with a transfer to a trust, the transfer of a deed subject to a life estate can trigger a Medicaid ineligibility period for up to five years. The value of the remainder interest is the amount of the gift and determines the period of ineligibility for institutional care. As the value of the remainder interest is often considerably less than the value of the home, this planning technique typically reduces the period of ineligibility quite significantly.

> **Example:** Jane gives a remainder interest in her house to her children, George and Mary, while retaining a life interest for herself. She carries this out by signing a simple deed that carves out a life estate for herself. Thereafter, Jane, the life estate holder, has the right to live in the property or rent it out, collecting the rents for herself. On the other hand, she is responsible for the costs of maintenance and taxes on the property. In addition, the property cannot be sold to a third party without the cooperation of George and Mary, the remainder interest holders.

Upon Jane's death, the house will not pass through probate, because at her death the ownership will pass automatically to the holders of the remainder interest, George and Mary. Although the property will not be included in Jane's probate estate, it will be included in her taxable estate [IRS Code Section 2036.] The downside of this is that depending on the size of the estate and the state's estate tax threshold, the property may be subject to estate taxation. Another downside is that if the home is sold during the lifetime of the life tenant, then Medicaid can count the value of the life estate at the time of the sale as an available asset for Medicaid purposes. The upside is that this can create a significant reduction in the capital gains tax imposed when George and Mary sell the property because they will receive a *step up* in the property's basis.

Life estates are created simply by executing a deed conveying the remainder interest to another while retaining a life interest, as Jane did in the above example. Once the house passes to George and Mary, the state cannot recover against it any Medicaid expenses Jane may have incurred.

Trusts

A better way to protect the home from estate recovery is to transfer it to an irrevocable trust. Trusts provide more flexibility than life estates, but they are somewhat more complicated. Once the house is transferred to the irrevocable trust, it cannot be removed. Although the home can be sold, the proceeds must remain in the trust. This can protect more of the value of the house if it is sold. Further, if properly drafted, the later sale of the home, while in this trust, might allow the settler (or grantor), if she has met the residency requirements, to exclude up to $250,000 in taxable gain—an exclusion that would not be available if the owner had transferred the home directly to a non-resident child or other third party before its sale.

Spending Down

Applicants for Medicaid and their spouses may protect their savings by spending them down on noncountable or exempt assets. These expenditures may include

- preparing funeral costs,
- paying off a mortgage,
- making repairs to a home,
- replacing an old automobile,
- updating home furnishings,
- paying for more care at home, or
- buying a new home.

In the case of married couples, it is often important that any spend-down steps be taken prior to the time the ill spouse moves to a nursing home if this would affect the community spouse's resource allowance.

Spousal Protections

Immediate Annuities

Immediate annuities can be ideal planning tools for spouses of nursing home residents. For single individuals, they are usually less useful. An immediate annuity, in its simplest form, is a contract with an insurance company under which the consumer pays a certain amount of money to the company and the company pays the consumer a monthly check for the rest of her life or for a period of time. In most states, the purchase of a properly structured annuity will not be considered a transfer for purposes of Medicaid eligibility, but will instead be treated as an investment. It transforms otherwise countable assets of the community spouse into a non-countable income stream. As long as the income is in the name of and payable to the community spouse, it will not pose a problem. However, certain states will require that the community spouse contribute a portion of the income towards the ill spouse's care.

> **Example:** Mr. Jones, the community spouse, lives in a state where the most money she can keep for herself and still have Mrs. Jones qualify for Medicaid nursing home care (his maximum resource allowance) is $104,400 (in 2008). However, Mr. Jones has $214,400 in countable assets. He can take the difference of $110,000 and purchase an irrevocable and non-assignable immediate annuity, making his wife in the nursing home immediately eligible for Medicaid. He would continue to receive the annuity check each month for the rest of his life, or for a period of time not exceeding his life expectancy.

In most instances, the purchase of an annuity by the community spouse should wait until the ill spouse moves to a nursing home. In addition, if the annuity has a term certain—a guaranteed number of payments no matter the lifespan of the annuitant—the term must be shorter than the life expectancy of the community spouse. Further, if the community spouse dies with guaranteed payments remaining on the annuity, the remaining payments must be payable to the state for reimbursement up to the amount of Medicaid paid for either spouse.

Annuities are of less benefit for a single individual in a nursing home because she would have to pay the monthly income from the annuity to the nursing home in any event.

In short, immediate annuities are a very powerful tool in the right circumstances. They must also be distinguished from deferred annuities, which have no Medicaid planning purpose.

An insurance company need not always become involved when annuities are used in a Medicaid context. Many states permit the use of a *private annuity*, where, for example, the children, rather than an insurance company, can act as the issuer of an immediate, irrevocable, and non-assignable annuity.

(The use of immediate annuities as a Medicaid planning tool is under attack in some states. Clients should consult with a qualified elder law attorney in the state in which they reside before pursuing the strategy described above.)

Increased Community Spouse Resource Allowance

Before passage of the DRA, in some states, community spouses with income less than the MMMNA had an alternative to merely receiving the shortfall from the income of the nursing home spouse. These community spouses could petition the state Medicaid agency to allow for an increase in their standard resource allowances (called the community spouse resource allowance, or CSRA) so that the additional funds could be invested in order to generate income to make up for the shortfall in the MMMNA. The DRA has limited this practice.

Under the new law, an increased resource allowance may only be granted to community spouses whose income is still not enough to reach the MMMNA after first receiving the income of the nursing home spouse. This is called the *income first* rule.

Spousal Refusal

Federal Medicaid law states that the community spouse can keep all of his assets by simply refusing to support the institutionalized spouse. This portion of the law, known as *spousal refusal*, is generally not used extensively anywhere except in New York. Under the law, if a spouse refuses to contribute his income, resources, or both toward the cost of care of a Medicaid applicant, the Medicaid agency is required to determine the eligibility of the nursing home spouse based solely on the ill spouse's income, resources, or both, as if the community spouse did not exist. In addition, in 2005, a federal appeals court upheld the right of the wife of a Connecticut nursing home resident to refuse to support her husband. The husband was able to qualify for Medicaid coverage, and assets that he had transferred to his wife were not counted in determining his eligibility.

After awarding Medicaid eligibility to the institutionalized spouse, the Medicaid agency then has the option of beginning a legal proceeding to force the community spouse to support the institutionalized spouse. However, this is not always done, and when such cases do go to court, the community spouse is sometimes allowed to keep enough resources to maintain his former standard of living. If the Medicaid agency chooses not to sue the community spouse for support, it can file a claim for reimbursement against the community spouse's estate following his death.

This *just say no* strategy sometimes is used in states other than New York in second-marriage situations, where the healthy spouse truly refuses to support the nursing home spouse.

Medicare

5

Medicare is the federal government's principal health care insurance program for people 65 years of age and over. The Medicare program insures 39 million Americans and spends $213 billion a year on their care. Medicare is an *entitlement* program, meaning it is not based on financial need.

Although Medicare was originally conceived as a program that would relieve older persons of the burden of paying for health care, Medicare beneficiaries now pay a *greater percentage* of their incomes for out-of-pocket health care expenses than they did before Medicare was enacted in 1965. In addition to paying a monthly premium, Medicare recipients are often required to pay a portion of the cost of the services they receive in the form of deductible or coinsurance amounts. Deductibles, coinsurance amounts, and premiums increase each January. In addition, there are many services and items, such as long-term nursing home or in-home care that Medicare does not cover. To help with this cost-sharing and the items that Medicare does not cover, Medicare beneficiaries often purchase private insurance policies called *Medigap* policies.

For the most part, Medicare pays only for *acute* care—care that the program's administrators view as reasonable and necessary to diagnose or treat an illness or injury. In other words, the program does not pay for most preventive or chronic health care. The program also covers people of any age who are permanently disabled or who have end-stage renal disease (people with kidney ailments that require dialysis or a kidney transplant).

Medicare consists of four major programs: Part A, which covers hospital stays; Part B, which covers physician fees; Part C, which permits Medicare beneficiaries to receive their medical care from among a number of delivery options; and the recently-added Part D, which covers prescription medications.

The topics that we will discuss in this chapter include the following:

- Medicare Part A
- Medicare Part B
- Home health benefits
- Medicare Part C
- Medicare managed care (Medicare Advantage)
- Prescription drug coverage (Medicare Part D)
- Appealing Medicare decisions
- Medigap policies

Medicare Part A

Medicare Part A is available for anyone who is over age 65 or who is permanently disabled *and* who is eligible for Social Security. Any person who has reached age 65 and who is entitled to Social Security benefits is eligible for Medicare Part A *without charge*. That is, there are no premiums for this part of the Medicare program.

Your client is eligible for Medicare Part A if he

- is a United States resident who has reached age 65 and is either a U.S. citizen or a legally admitted alien who has resided in the U.S. continuously for at least five years;
- is a disabled person of any age who has been entitled to Social Security, widower benefits, or Railroad Retirement disability benefits for 25 months; or
- has end-stage renal disease that requires dialysis treatment or a kidney transplant.

Medicare Part A covers institutional care in hospitals and skilled nursing facilities, as well as certain care given by home health agencies and care provided in hospices.

Hospital Coverage

Medicare pays for 90 days of hospital care per *spell of illness*, plus an additional lifetime reserve of 60 days. A single spell of illness begins when the patient is admitted to a hospital or other covered facility and ends when the patient has gone 60 days without being readmitted to a hospital or other facility. There is no limit on the number of spells of illness. However, the patient must satisfy a deductible, the amount of which changes annually, before Medicare begins paying for treatment.

After the deductible is satisfied, Medicare will pay for virtually all hospital charges during the first 60 days of a recipient's hospital stay, other than telephone and television expenses. What Medicare covers includes the following:

- a bed in a semiprivate room (meaning a room with at least one other patient as Medicare will pay for a private room only if it is *medically necessary*)
- all meals
- regular nursing services
- operating room, intensive care unit, or coronary care unit charges
- medical supplies
- drugs furnished by the hospital
- laboratory tests
- x-rays
- the use of appliances
- medical social services
- physical and occupational therapy
- speech therapy
- blood transfusions after the first three pints of blood

Medicare will *not* pay for treatments or procedures that it considers medically unproven or experimental.

If the hospital stay extends beyond 60 days, the Medicare beneficiary begins shouldering more of the cost of his care. From day 61 through day 90, the patient pays coinsurance. Beyond the 90th day, the patient begins to tap into his 60-day lifetime reserve. During hospital stays covered by these reserve days, beneficiaries must pay coinsurance. This reserve is not reset after each spell of illness. Once it has been exhausted, the beneficiary will receive coverage for only 90 days when the next spell of illness occurs. However, studies show that the average length of a hospital stay covered by Medicare is eight days.

Medicare Part A also pays for stays in psychiatric hospitals, but payment is limited to a total of 190 days of inpatient psychiatric hospital services during a beneficiary's lifetime.

Fighting a Hospital Discharge

If your client is admitted to a hospital as a Medicare patient, the hospital may try to discharge him before he is ready. He may need more time to recover from surgery or accident, but the hospital may want the room back. While the hospital can't force your client to leave, it can begin charging him for services. Therefore, it is important for your client to know his rights and to know how to appeal. Even if he does not win the appeal, appealing can buy him crucial extra days of Medicare coverage.

Before a hospital can discharge your client, it must give him a written notice of discharge. If he does not receive a notice and the hospital is threatening to discharge him or begins charging him for services, he can ask for the hospital to give him its discharge decision in writing. Your client can't appeal the discharge until he receives the notice—called a Hospital-Issued Notice of Non-coverage or Notice of Discharge and Medicare Appeal Rights—in writing.

Once your client receives a notice, he should immediately contact his local Medicare *Quality Improvement Organization (QIO)*. A QIO is a group of doctors and other professionals who monitor quality of care. They are paid by the federal government and not affiliated with a hospital or health maintenance organization (HMO). The telephone number should be on the notice.

It is very important to contact the QIO right away. In fact, your client must contact the QIO by noon on the first business day after he receives the notice. If he does this, he will not have to pay for his care while he waits for his discharge to be reviewed. If he doesn't contact the QIO by noon, the hospital can begin charging him on the third day after he receives the notice.

The QIO will conduct a review of the discharge. The QIO doctors will review the medical necessity, appropriateness, and the quality of hospital treatment furnished to your client. The hospital cannot discharge your client while the QIO is reviewing the discharge decision, and your client will not have to pay for the additional days in the hospital. If your client doesn't agree with the QIO's decision, he can then ask it to reconsider. It must issue a decision within three days.

If, after the reconsideration, the QIO still agrees with the hospital's decision, your client can appeal to an administrative law judge (ALJ). Your client will probably need legal counsel to help him through this process. He can appeal the ALJ's decision to the Department of Health and Human Services' Departmental Appeals Board (DAB) if the ALJ rules against him. Finally, if your client doesn't agree with the DAB decision, he can appeal to federal court as long as at least $1,000 is at stake.

Skilled Nursing Facility Coverage

Medicare Part A covers up to 100 days of *skilled nursing* care per spell of illness. However, the conditions for obtaining Medicare coverage of a nursing home stay are quite stringent. The following are the main requirements:

1. The Medicare recipient must enter the nursing home no more than 30 days after a hospital stay that itself lasted for at least three days (not counting the day of discharge).
2. The care provided in the nursing home must be for the same condition that caused the hospitalization (or a condition medically related to it).
3. The patient must receive a skilled level of care in the nursing facility that cannot be provided at home or on an outpatient basis. In order to be considered skilled, nursing care must be ordered by a physician and delivered by or under the supervision of a professional such as a physical therapist, registered nurse, or licensed practical nurse. Moreover, such care must be delivered on a daily basis. (Few nursing home residents receive this level of care.)

As soon as the nursing facility determines that a patient is no longer receiving a skilled level of care, the Medicare coverage ends. And, beginning on day 21 of the nursing home stay, there is a significant copayment equal to one-eighth of the initial hospital deductible. This copayment can usually be covered by a Medigap insurance policy, provided the patient has one.

A new spell of illness can begin if the patient has not received skilled care, either in a skilled nursing facility (SNF) or in a hospital, for a period of 60 consecutive days. The patient, thus, can remain in the SNF and still qualify for Medicare as long as he does not receive a skilled level of care during those 60 days.

Nursing homes often terminate Medicare coverage for SNF care before they should. Two misunderstandings most often result in inappropriate denial of Medicare coverage to SNF patients. First, many nursing homes assume in error that if a patient has stopped making progress towards recovery then Medicare coverage should end. In fact, if the patient needs continued skilled care simply to maintain his status (or to slow deterioration) then the care should be provided and is covered by Medicare.

Second, nursing homes may wrongly believe that care requiring only supervision (rather than direct administration) by a skilled nurse is excluded from Medicare's SNF benefit. In fact, patients often receive an array of treatments that do not need to be carried out by a skilled nurse but which may, in combination, require skilled supervision. In these instances, if the potential for adverse interactions among multiple treatments requires that a skilled nurse monitor the patient's care and status, then Medicare will continue to provide coverage.

When a patient leaves a hospital and moves to a nursing home that provides Medicare coverage, the nursing home must give the patient written notice stating it believes that the patient requires a skilled level of care and thus merits Medicare coverage. Even in cases where the SNF initially treats the patient as a Medicare recipient, after two or more weeks the SNF will often determine that the patient no longer needs a skilled level of care and will issue a *Notice of Non-Coverage* terminating the Medicare coverage.

Whether the non-coverage determination is provided upon entering the SNF or after a period of treatment, the notice asks whether the patient would like the nursing home bill to be submitted to Medicare despite the nursing home's assessment of his care needs. The patient (or his guardian) should always ask for the bill to be submitted. This requires the nursing home to submit the patient's medical records for review to the fiscal intermediary, an insurance company hired by Medicare that reviews the facility's determination.

The review costs the patient nothing and may result in more Medicare coverage. While the review is being conducted, the patient is not obligated to pay the nursing home. However, if the appeal is denied, the patient will owe the facility retroactively for the period under review.

If the fiscal intermediary agrees with the nursing home that the patient no longer requires a skilled level of care, the next level of appeal is to an ALJ. This appeal may take a year and involves hiring a lawyer. It should be pursued only if, after reviewing the patient's medical records, the lawyer believes that the patient was receiving a skilled level of care that should have been covered by Medicare. If your client is turned down at this appeal level, there can be subsequent appeals to the Appeals Council in Washington, DC, and then to federal court.

Hospice Care

If the Medicare beneficiary is diagnosed as having no more than six months to live, Medicare will pay for unlimited hospice care. This can be at home or in a hospice facility, and includes services not generally covered by Medicare. These services include home health aide and homemaker services, physical therapy, and counseling, as well as physician and nursing services. There is also a provision for *respite care*—up to five consecutive days of inpatient care to give the patient's primary at-home caregiver some relief. The patient must pay 5 percent of the cost of this respite care.

Hospice benefit recipients are responsible for up to a $5 copayment for each prescription drug, but otherwise there are no deductibles or other copayments for this benefit. Bear in mind, however, that in electing hospice care, the beneficiary is choosing to receive noncurative medical and support services rather than treatment toward a cure for the terminal illness.

Because Medicare's hospice home care benefits do not cover full-time care, it is not an option unless there is a full-time caretaker in the home.

Medicare Part B

Medicare Part B is available for anyone over age 65 regardless of Social Security eligibility. Part B basically covers *outpatient* care: Office visits to medical specialists, ambulance transportation, diagnostic tests performed in a doctor's office or in a hospital on an outpatient basis, physician visits while the patient is in the hospital, and various outpatient therapies that are prescribed by a physician. Part B also covers a number of preventive services. In addition, Part B covers home health services if the beneficiary is not enrolled in Medicare Part A. (See the "Home Health Benefits" section in this chapter.)

Medicare recipients who are eligible for Part A are automatically enrolled in Part B unless they opt out. Part B enrollees pay a monthly premium that is adjusted annually. This premium, which is $96.40 a month in 2008, pays for about a quarter of Part B's actual costs; the federal government pays for the other 75 percent through general tax revenues. This cost-sharing makes Part B somewhat of a bargain, and many Medicare recipients buy it unless their present or former employer provides comparable coverage.

Beginning in January 2007, higher income beneficiaries paid higher Part B premiums. Table 5.1 shows the higher premium rates for 2008.

Table 5.1: Medicare Part B Premiums for 2008

Individual Annual Income	Married-Couple Annual Income	Monthly Premium
$82,000–$102,000	$164,000–$204,000	$122.20
$102,000–$153,000	$204,000–$306,000	$160.90
$153,00–$205,000 or more	$306,00–$410,00	$199.70
$205,000 or more	$410,000 or more	$238.40

There is a significant financial incentive not to delay enrollment; those who wait to enroll in Part B until after they become eligible for Medicare must pay a penalty. For each year that an individual puts off enrolling, his monthly premium increases by 10 percent—permanently. Thus, a person who waits five years to enroll in Part B will pay premiums 50 percent higher than he would otherwise. (This penalty does not apply if the individual is covered by an employer group plan that is available only to current employees.)

The specifics of what is covered and what is not covered under Part B are complex and change periodically in response to efforts to contain health care costs. The following are some of the items that are *excluded* from coverage:

- prescription drugs that are not administered by a physician
- routine physical checkups
- eye glasses or contact lenses (in most cases)

- hearing aids
- orthopedic shoes, except for diabetics
- custodial care
- cosmetic surgery
- immunizations except pneumococcal vaccines
- most dental services
- routine foot care

Medicare Part B recipients must satisfy an annual deductible of $135 (in 2008). Once the deductible has been met, Medicare pays 80 percent of what Medicare considers a "reasonable charge" for the item or service. The beneficiary is responsible for the other 20 percent.

In most cases, however, what Medicare calls a *reasonable charge* is less than what a doctor or other medical provider normally charges for a service. A Medicare beneficiary's obligation to pay part of the difference between the Medicare-approved charge and the provider's normal charge depends on whether or not the provider has agreed to participate in the Medicare program.

If the provider participates in the Medicare program, he *accepts assignment*, which means that the provider agrees that the total charge for the covered service will be the amount approved by Medicare. Medicare then pays the provider 80 percent of its approved amount, after subtracting any part of the beneficiary's annual deductible that has not already been met. The provider then charges the beneficiary the remaining 20 percent of the approved reasonable charge, plus any part of the deductible that has not been satisfied.

Some states either require all licensed physicians to participate in the Medicare program or require even nonparticipating providers to accept the Medicare-approved rate as full payment.

But many states have no such requirements. If a Medicare beneficiary in one of these states is treated by a nonparticipating provider who is charging more than the Medicare-approved rate, the beneficiary must pay the usual 20 percent of the Medicare-approved charge *plus* an additional 15 percent of the Medicare-approved amount, which is called a *limiting charge*.

Note: It is against the law for providers in any state to charge Medicare patients more than an additional 15 percent of the Medicare-approved charge.

> **Example:** Doctor Jones bills Mrs. Smith $150 for an office visit that Medicare says should cost only $100. Mrs. Smith must pay Dr. Jones $35—20 percent of the approved charge ($20) plus an additional 15 percent of the approved charge ($15).
>
> In such *non-assignment* cases, Medicare pays the beneficiary 80 percent of the approved amount and the beneficiary must pay the provider the entire charge that is due. In this example, however, not all of the charges are due: Doctor Jones is taking a loss (compared to his standard rate) of $35 in treating Mrs. Smith. Doctor Jones must accept this loss as the price of treating a Medicare patient.

Other physician practices that violate Medicare Part B's rules include the following:

- requiring patients to waive their right to Medicare benefits and making them pay privately for Medicare-covered services
- requiring beneficiaries to pay for services such as telephone conversations with the doctor, prescription refills, and medical conferences with other professionals for which they were never previously charged
- requiring beneficiaries to sign a paper agreeing to pay privately for all services that Medicare will not cover and then using this waiver to make beneficiaries pay for a service that Medicare covers as part of a package of related procedures
- suing beneficiaries in small claims court for amounts above the 15 percent *limiting* charge
- billing for services that do not have a set fee and claiming that no charge limits apply to these services

Medicare patients do not have to share the cost of *all* services under Medicare Part B. Medicare pays for certain services in full, including diagnostic laboratory tests, home health services, second opinions on surgery (or third opinions if the two earlier opinions disagree), expenses for pneumococcal vaccine, and costs to kidney transplant donors. In all these cases, the $135 (in 2008) deductible does not apply and the 20 percent copayment is waived. On the other hand, Medicare will pay only 50 percent of the approved rate for the treatment of mental disorders on an outpatient basis.

Home Health Benefits

If your client qualifies, Medicare will cover his home health care benefits entirely, and though under the law there is no limit to the length of time he will be covered, in practice, coverage is limited.

Nevertheless, Medicare home health benefits can mean the difference between your client or client's family member continuing to stay at home or his health deteriorating until hospital care or nursing home placement becomes necessary.

Your client is entitled to Medicare coverage of his home health care if he meets the following requirements:

- if he is confined to his home (meaning that leaving it to receive services would be a *considerable and taxing effort*)
- if his doctor has ordered home health services for him
- if at least some element of the services he receives is *skilled* (intermittent skilled nursing care, physical therapy, or speech therapy)

What your client receives: If your client requires an element of skilled care, then he will also be entitled to Medicare coverage of social services, part-time or intermittent home health aide services, and necessary medical supplies and durable medical equipment. Your client can receive up to 35 hours of services a week, although few beneficiaries actually get this level of service. Your client is entitled to the same level of services whether he is a member of an HMO or is enrolled in traditional fee-for-service Medicare.

What your client pays: Your client will not have to pay anything, with the exception of 20 percent of the cost of medical supplies and equipment, which is covered by some Medigap policies.

While the government insists that it has not changed the criteria for who is eligible for home care services, home health agencies have invariably cut back on services they provide in order to balance their own budgets .

This means that Medicare recipients must advocate for the services they need. If your client has to appeal a termination of service, the good news is that most people who appeal Medicare home health benefits win their cases. At the first level of review, 39 percent are successful, and on appeal to an administrative law judge, 81 percent are successful. The bad news is that your client has to pay privately for the care in order to have an issue that is able to be appealed. This is because the issue of appeal is not the termination of a service, but the denial of Medicare payment for the service. As a result, many beneficiaries simply try to make do without the care or hire help on their own without the training and supervision provided by home health agencies.

Most Medicare beneficiaries are not informed of their appellate rights when given notice that their home health care benefits will be terminated. Attorneys have filed a nationwide class action suit on behalf of homebound seniors seeking advance notice of any termination of benefits for Medicare home health coverage, as well as notice of the ability to appeal such a denial before the termination occurs. If your client's benefits or those of his family members are reduced or terminated, you should advise your client to take the following steps:

1. Ask his home health agency to provide an explanation of the cutback in writing. Ask the agency to give written notice of the cutback or termination of service.
2. Ask his physician to call the agency to urge it not to cutback the services and to provide a letter verifying the level of care he needs. This can be essential to whether he ultimately receives the benefits he deserves.
3. Consult his attorney or a Medicare assistance agency in his state to determine whether an appeal would be successful.
4. If he decides to appeal, he should do so immediately, and make arrangements with the home health agency to pay privately for the services pending the result of the appeal.

Medicare Part C

Medicare beneficiaries may choose to receive coverage from HMOs, fee-for-service Medicare, and a menu of options (at least on paper) that includes the following:

- **Preferred Provider Organizations (PPOs).** Networks that allow the use of doctors and hospitals outside the plan network for an extra out-of-pocket cost.
- **Provider Sponsored Organizations (PSOs).** Networks established by doctors and hospitals.

- **Private fee-for-service plans.** Medicare-approved private health insurance plans for which Medicare pays part of the cost. Plans would provide an unlimited choice of providers and could charge unlimited premiums.
- **Medical Savings Account (MSA) plans.** Plans that offer a way for Medicare recipients to opt out of the federal program altogether and reap some savings if they stay healthy. Each year, Medicare would give an enrollee a voucher equal to the average annual cost of treating a Medicare beneficiary. The enrollee would use part of the voucher's value to purchase a private health insurance policy with a high deductible (not to exceed $6,000), called a *catastrophic* policy. The remainder of the voucher's value could be invested in a tax-free MSA, which would be available to pay for any treatment costs. If the recipient stays healthy, he can pocket money left in the account. The MSA option is currently a demonstration program available to up to 390,000 Medicare enrollees.
- **Special contracts.** Beneficiaries who so desire may enter contractual agreements for specific services with physicians who have agreed not to participate in Medicare for two years. Medicare would not pay any part of the cost for these services and there are *no limits on what the physician can charge.*

Until 2002, Medicare beneficiaries were able to switch among traditional Medicare and these other new options easily, typically with just a month's notice. However, now nine months' notice is usually required before switching. But beneficiaries who are happy with the way they are receiving Medicare can stay with that program, unless the program stops participating in Medicare. New Medicare enrollees who do not choose a particular program will automatically be enrolled in traditional Medicare.

The Medicare Prescription Drug, Improvement, and Modernization Act, enacted in 2003, changed the name of these private Medicare alternatives to Medicare Advantage and raised payment levels to local plans and would-be regional PPOs.

Medicare Managed Care (Medicare Advantage)

We have all heard about managed care, and many of us have first-hand experience with this new health care arrangement. Managed care is a strategy to reduce health care costs by discouraging providers from performing unneeded services and by promoting preventive medicine.

The basic thrust of managed care is that a health plan is paid a flat monthly fee for each patient under its care. If the plan's costs in caring for that patient are less than the fixed fee, the plan makes money. But if the patient is quite sick and requires many costly medical services, then the plan may lose money on that particular patient. In this way, plans have an investment in keeping costs down.

When Medicare costs started skyrocketing along with the rest of the health care sector, Congress looked to managed care as a partial remedy. As a consequence, the Medicare program now contracts with managed care plans to provide services to Medicare beneficiaries who choose the managed care option (now called Medicare Advantage). The managed care plan receives a fixed monthly fee to provide services to each Medicare beneficiary under its care. As a Medicare managed care enrollee, your client receives all the coverage he would receive under regular Medicare, except without the large copayments and deductibles he would normally pay. In addition, your client often receives coverage for products and services that Medicare does not cover, such as prescription drugs or custodial care. Generally, your client does not need a supplemental Medigap policy if he joins a managed care plan. Sound too good to be true? In a way, it is as there are restrictions in a managed care plan, discussed in the following section.

Restrictions on Providers and Services

First, managed care plans keep their costs down by limiting a patient's freedom to choose which doctors and other providers the patient can see. The most prominent type of managed care plan, the HMO, maintains a list or network of health care providers (doctors, hospitals, etc.) that its patients are allowed to use. The plan has negotiated special rates with these network providers. If a member uses the services of a provider who is not in the network, the plan will not pay the bill, and neither will Medicare.

If a managed care plan your client is considering joining restricts access to providers, it is important to determine whether his doctors and other providers he wishes to see are in the plan's network. But bear in mind that managed care plans drop providers from their networks if they start costing the plan too much money. So just because your client's doctor is a member of the network now doesn't guarantee that he will be part of the network later.

Another way plans strive to reduce costs is by requiring that all care be funneled through a primary care physician. This doctor makes all the decisions about whether or not to refer the patient to a specialist, so your client wouldn't be able to make an appointment with a specialist on his own. The primary care physician is strongly encouraged to take care of all medical problems himself and refer your client to a specialist only when absolutely necessary. Medicare does require, however, that managed care plans allow patients with serious conditions, such as heart disease, kidney failure and cancer, to see specialists without referrals from their primary care physicians. Also, routine preventive women's health care screening must be available without a referral.

For many, managed care's most disagreeable cost-cutting strategy is the common requirement that your client's primary care physician obtain the plan's approval before he can receive certain medical services. If the plan administrators disagree with your client's physician that a procedure is medically necessary, the plan may refuse to pay for it. Plans also attempt to reduce costs by allowing their members shorter periods of hospital and nursing home care than Medicare beneficiaries generally receive. In addition, managed care plans provide fewer rehabilitative services like home health care and outpatient therapies than traditional Medicare provides.

Not all managed care plans are so restrictive, but the less restrictive plans are more expensive. Some offer what is known as a *point of service* option that allows your client to see physicians or other providers that are not in the network. If your client goes outside of the network, however, he will pay a higher portion of the bill than if he saw an in-network physician.

Given the restrictions of managed care, if your client is considering joining a particular plan, it is a good idea to talk with his doctor about his experiences with that plan. How does the plan handle approving treatments, referring patients to specialists, or allowing patients to remain in the hospital if they are not ready to leave? Does the plan frequently overrule the doctor? Your client might also want to ask the same questions regarding the doctor's billing staff.

The True Cost of Medicare Managed Care

Given all these restrictions, one would think that managed care would cost less than a Medigap policy. While many managed care plans charge patients no premium over and above the Medicare Part B premium, others, such as those offering a point of service option or unlimited prescription drug coverage, charge a small additional premium.

In addition, patients may be responsible for copayments. These are charges plan members must pay out of pocket when they receive certain kinds of care, such as an office visit or a prescription drug. The copayment usually ranges from $5 to $15, depending on the managed care plan. If your client sees a lot of doctors or takes an array of prescribed medications, the costs can add up. The plan may also only cover medications listed in its *formulary*—the list of drugs it approves. For drugs not in the formulary, the copayment may be higher or the plan may pay nothing at all. Bear in mind that managed care plans often change the drugs in their formulary, so a medication currently covered now may not be covered at a later date.

Another consideration is the extent of the plan's service area. If your client's plan's service area is limited, he may lack access to a broad range of providers.

On the positive side, managed care plans may offer coverage that goes well beyond regular Medicare coverage, including the following:

- 100 percent coverage of needed medical equipment
- Chiropractic care, acupuncture, and acupressure
- Foreign travel coverage
- Eye examinations
- Dental work
- Hearing tests and hearing aids
- After-hours care

Comparison Shop Online

A great source of information for those trying to negotiate the managed care maze is the *Health Insurance Counseling and Advocacy Program* (HICAP). This independent group, which is funded by state agencies on aging and by private donations, counsels seniors about Medicare managed care and Medigap policies available to them in their area. HICAP offices have a different (usually toll free "800") main number in each state.

You can also advise your clients to contact their *State Health Insurance Assistance Program* (SHIP). The telephone number for the SHIP in your client's state is available by calling 1-800-MEDICARE (1-800-633-4227). SHIP volunteers are available to discuss your client's individual situation and provide information on options available to him.

Appealing Managed Care Plan Decisions

Your client's plan may overrule his doctor and refuse to cover a treatment or procedure that it deems to be medically unnecessary or experimental. By one count, nearly one-third of Medicare managed care plan enrollees maintain they were denied coverage for treatment by their plans. Such denials of coverage can be enraging or even life-threatening. If your client's plan will not pay for, does not allow, or stops a service that your client thinks should be covered or provided, your client can file an appeal. However, this appeals process is run by the plan. After your client files the appeal, the plan will review its decision. If the plan does not decide in your client's favor, the appeal can be reviewed by an independent organization.

Medicare managed care beneficiaries sued the Medicare program, claiming that it was not adequately protecting their right to appeal adverse decisions by managed care plans. This suit was settled and resulted in new regulations that strengthen Medicare beneficiaries' appellate rights under managed care. Medicare must now require managed care plans to let patients know four days before it will stop covering their home health, nursing home, or certain outpatient rehabilitation care. This advance written notice must explain

- why the HMO thinks that services are either not needed or are not covered;
- how patients can go about obtaining a fast appeal of the decision from an independent decision maker outside the HMO if they think the services are covered; and
- that payment for the costs of patient care will continue at least until noon of the day following the decision by the independent decision maker.

Medicare officials are also revising some of the requirements covering managed care organizations that terminate hospital services for Medicare beneficiaries.

Your client should check his plan's membership materials or contact the plan for details about his appellate rights.

Entering and Leaving Medicare Managed Care

Your client must be enrolled in Medicare Part A and Part B before he can enroll in a Medicare managed care plan. If he wants to join a Medicare managed care plan, he should contact the plan and ask if it is accepting new member enrollments or if it has a waiting list. Plans must accept your client if he applies within the first six months of signing up for both Parts A and B of Medicare. They also must enroll your client during the open enrollment month of November for coverage beginning January 1. Some plans have continuous open enrollment, meaning that they will accept Medicare beneficiaries at any time. In addition, the Tax Relief and Health Care Act of 2006 allows people with original Medicare to join a Medicare Advantage Plan that does not include Medicare prescription drug coverage outside of the normal enrollment periods at any time in 2007 or 2008. Note, however, if your client has Medicare prescription drug coverage, it will be cancelled if he joins a Medicare Advantage Plan without coverage.

Managed care plans do not always have to accept new enrollments, however. Some plans have approved limits on the number of beneficiaries they can enroll (called *capacity limits*). Once a plan has reached its capacity limit, it does not have to accept any new enrollments. Still, if a managed care plan refuses to accept your client's enrollment, it must provide a written denial.

It is fairly easy to leave a managed care plan and return to regular Medicare if your client so chooses. He can leave a plan in one of three ways:

- Call the plan he wishes to leave and ask for an un-enrollment form
- Call 1-800-MEDICARE (1-800-633-4227) to request that his un-enrollment be processed over the telephone
- Call the Social Security Administration or visit his Social Security Office to file his un-enrolled request

In most cases, your client is un-enrolled the month after his request is made as long as his request was filed before the tenth day of the month. If his request was made after the tenth of the month, he will be un-enrolled the first day of the second calendar month after his request was made.

Your client need not fill out an un-enrollment form if he decides to join another managed care plan. He will be automatically un-enrolled from his old plan when his new plan enrollment becomes effective.

After your client leaves Medicare managed care, he automatically returns to the regular Medicare program. It is very likely he will be able to continue seeing the same doctors and providers he was seeing in the managed care plan, if this is his wish.

Prescription Drug Coverage (Medicare Part D)

The first-ever federally subsidized drug program for seniors, in which private health insurers offer limited insurance coverage of prescription drugs to elderly and disabled Medicare recipients, took effect on January 1, 2006. The new drug benefit will be available only through insurers that contract with Medicare to market drug plans.

What Does the New Drug Benefit Cost and What Do Members Get?

Medicare recipients who elect to be covered by the new drug benefit will pay premiums averaging $27.93 a month in 2008. This is an average; some plans will charge more, some less.

After meeting a $275 (in 2008) deductible, members will pay 25 percent of drug costs up to $2,510 (in 2008) in a year, with Medicare footing the bill for the other 75 percent. The plan will pay $1,682.25 and members will pay $558.75. Coverage will then stop completely until total spending for covered drugs reaches $4,050 (in 2008). (This coverage gap is sometimes called the *doughnut hole*.) In other words, after a member reaches the $2,510 limit noted above, he will be responsible for covering the next $3,216.25 (in 2008) in drug costs himself. Once total spending for his covered drugs exceeds $5,726.25, coverage will kick back in, with Medicare paying about 95 percent of costs above $5,726.25 (called *catastrophic coverage*).

This means that beneficiaries must have $4,050 in out-of-pocket costs in 2008 to reach the $5,726.25 threshold, at which point the program's catastrophic coverage takes effect. This $4,050 figure is the sum of the $275 deductible plus 25 percent of costs up to $2,510 ($558.75) plus the $3,216.25 that must be spent before members can get out of the doughnut hole. One way to avoid the coverage gap is to pick a plan with low drug prices, since it is accumulating drug costs that bring members closer to the gap—not low premiums, copayments, or deductibles. (We are describing Medicare's basic prescription drug coverage, which all insurers must offer. Insurers may also offer more generous coverage and charge a higher premium for it.)

Bear in mind that only payments for drugs that are covered by your client's plan (see "What Drugs Are Covered" below) count towards the out-of-pocket threshold. Also, any help with paying for Medicare Part D costs that your client receives from an employer health plan or other insurance does not count toward this limit. Drugs purchased abroad (such as from Canada) will not be covered by the Medicare benefit and will not count toward the out-of-pocket limit.

What Do Members Save?

AARP, which used its considerable political might to assure passage of the new drug benefit, has created a calculator for beneficiaries to determine their potential savings under Medicare Part D. To use the calculator, visit www.aarp.org and do a search for "Medicare Drug Benefit Calculator." (Note that the calculations apply only to individuals who pay 100 percent of their prescription drug costs. Results will not be accurate for low-income Medicare beneficiaries or for those who currently have some form of prescription drug coverage.)

What Drugs Are Covered?

All Part D enrollees will have at least two Medicare private drug plans to choose from, and in most areas a number of plans. The insurers may choose the medicines—both brand-name and generic—that they will include in a plan's formulary. However, each plan formulary must include at least two drugs in each drug class and must cover a majority of the drugs in certain classes, such as antidepressants and anti-cancer agents.

Since each drug plan will offer a different formulary, and the same drug may vary in price from plan to plan, the most important job for a Medicare beneficiary signing up for Part D is to determine whether the prescription drugs he needs—or anticipates needing—will be covered under a particular plan and how much they will cost. In most regions, there will be no shortage of choices. California, for example, is projected to have 40 plans competing for business.

Plans will differ in the monthly premiums they charge, deductibles, the drugs they cover, the cost of those drugs, limitations on drug purchases, and the convenience of the plan's pharmacy network, among other factors. A comparison tool is available on Medicare's Web site (www.medicare.gov) that allows your client to search for Medicare private drug plans in his region and compare their costs, covered drugs, and pharmacy networks. The information is also available by calling 1-800-MEDICARE. In addition, the *Medicare & You 2008* handbook provides information about the Medicare private drug plans in your client's area. (Available at http://www.medicare.gov). Your client can also visit the Elder Law Answers Web site (www.elderlawanswers.com) for a Drug Plan Comparison Worksheet that allows beneficiaries to note important information about each plan, compare the plans side by side, and identify the one that best meets their needs.

But it is possible that all of your client's diligent research could come to nothing because after he has enrolled in what seems to be the best plan, the plan may discontinue coverage or increase the cost of any particular drug! Can your client then switch plans? Only those eligible for both Medicare and Medicaid (see the section "What If Your Client is Enrolled in Both Medicare and Medicaid?" further on in this chapter for more information) may switch plans whenever they want. Other beneficiaries will be locked into their choice for a full year; however, your client will not lose coverage for any drugs he is currently taking.

If a company drops coverage for a drug, it must continue to cover participants currently taking that drug until the end of the year. There are some exceptions—for example, if the drug is determined to be unsafe or a lower-cost generic drug comes on the market.

Medicare Part D does not cover certain drugs, including barbiturates and benzodiazepines, which are prescribed for older people to treat insomnia, seizure disorders, anxiety, panic attacks, and muscle spasms.

States have the option of providing Medicaid coverage for the excluded drugs.

Each Medicare drug plan will likely give your client a list of local pharmacies where he can obtain his covered drugs.

Who May Enroll?

Anyone who has either Medicare Part A or Medicare Part B (or both) can enroll in Medicare Part D, Medicare's prescription drug coverage. Bear in mind, however, that Medicare Part D will not pay for drugs that could have been paid for under Medicare Part A or Medicare Part B. These drugs will not be covered even if the beneficiary does not have either Part A or Part B.

How Does Your Client Enroll?

Once your client has chosen the Medicare private drug plan he wants to enroll in, he can contact the company offering the plan and ask for a paper application, or he may complete an on-line application on the plan's Web site, if the plan allows on-line applications. The on-line application also may be available on Medicare's Web site, www.medicare.gov.

If your client cannot enroll himself, a representative who is authorized under state law can enroll for him. This could include a health care proxy, an agent acting under a power of attorney, or another surrogate decision maker as defined by state law.

If your client is in a Medicare HMO or PPO, he can enroll in a plan offered by the company that sponsors his Medicare health plan.

Late Enrollment Penalties

Medicare beneficiaries may be subject to significant financial penalties for late enrollment. For every month enrollees delay enrollment past the Initial Enrollment Period, the Medicare Part D premium will increase at least 1 percent. For example, if the average national premium in 2007 is $40 a month and your client delays enrollment for 15 months, his premium penalty would be $6 (1 percent x 15 x $40 = $6), meaning that he would pay $46 a month, not $40, for coverage that year and an extra $6 a month each succeeding year.

Beneficiaries are exempt from these penalties if they did not enroll because they had drug coverage from a private insurer, such as through a retirement plan, which was at least as good as Medicare's. This is called *creditable* coverage. Your client's insurer should have let him know if his coverage will be considered creditable.

Subsidies for Low-Income Beneficiaries

Assistance for low-income Medicare beneficiaries is available to help them pay the premiums, deductibles, copayments and coverage gap of the new drug benefit. In fact, the new program offers the greatest benefit to those with the lowest incomes, who could pay next-to-nothing for their drugs. For more on this, visit the Elder Law Answers Web site at www.elderlawanswers.com.

What If Your Client is Enrolled in Both Medicare and Medicaid?

Many low-income individuals have coverage under both Medicare and Medicaid. Medicaid had been covering prescription drugs for these *dual eligibles*, but the new law changed that. Beginning January 1, 2006, Medicaid stopped covering prescription drugs. Therefore, unlike other Medicare recipients who had until May 15, 2006, to enroll in a prescription drug plan, individuals covered by both Medicare and Medicaid had to enroll by January 1, 2006.

If dual eligibles did not enroll themselves, the Department of Health and Human Services automatically enrolled them in a plan. If your client had original Medicare, he would have been enrolled in a stand-alone drug plan whose premium is at or below the standard plan premium in his area. If he had an HMO or PPO, he would have been enrolled in the lowest premium prescription drug plan offered by that company.

If your client is a dual eligible, he should make sure the plan he was assigned to covers the drugs he needs and the pharmacies he frequents. If it does not, he will need to choose a different plan. Advise him to call 1-800-MEDICARE or go to www.medicare.gov to compare plans.

If your client is a dual eligible enrolled in a drug plan that stops covering a drug he needs, he can change his drug plan once a month. As noted above, other beneficiaries are locked into their choice for a full year.

What If Your Client Already Gets Retiree Drug Coverage from His Former Employer?

Clients must be advised to exercise extreme caution. If your client signs up for Medicare Part D, he will lose his company's retiree drug coverage, and some companies will cancel his medical insurance as well. If your client's retiree drug coverage is *creditable*—that is, if it is equal to or better than what Medicare is offering—then your client will not have to pay a late-enrollment penalty if he decides to switch to Medicare Part D at a later point in time. In other words, there is no rush and your client should be warned not to let a salesperson steamroll him into signing up for Medicare's benefit. Even if it is not creditable, he still needs to carefully consider his options. If he signs up for a Medicare drug plan and loses his medical insurance in the process, he may not be able to get it back. Before he signs up, advise him to ask his employer if he can drop his drug coverage without losing his other supplemental insurance. He should have received a letter stating whether or not his former employer's plan's coverage is creditable.

Caution: If a caller is stating they're with Social Security, your client should verify the call by contacting the agency at 1-800-772-1213.

For More Information

The new Medicare drug benefit is a complicated program (the program's rules and explanatory materials run to 1,172 pages). No single article can address all the questions or issues that beneficiaries may have. The following are some sources for more detailed information:

The National Citizens' Coalition for Nursing Home Reform (NCC-NHR) has developed two new consumer fact sheets on Medicare Part D, one for nursing home residents and one for assisted living residents. These fact sheets help consumers understand the who, what, and where of Medicare Part D in consumer-friendly language. They are in a question and answer format and can be accessed via the NCCNHR Web site at www.nccnhr.org. Table 5.2 illustrates other resources that may be of help to clients.

Table 5.2: Other Medicare Resources

Resource	*URL or Telephone*
2008 Medicare & You Handbook, The Facts About Medicare Prescription Drug Plans. Centers for Medicare & Medicaid Services	www.medicare.gov
Medicare Drug Coverage 101: Everything You Need to Know About the New Medicare Prescription DrugBenefit. The Medicare Rights Center	www.medicarerights.org*
The New Medicare Prescription Drug Coverage: What You Need to Know and AARP's Drug Benefit Calculator.	www.aarp.org
Definitions of Selected Health Insurance Terminology Under Medicare Part D, Medigap Update. Center for Medicare Advocacy, Inc.	www.medicareadvocacy.org
Resources on the Medicare Prescription Drug Benefit. Kaiser Family Foundation	www.kff.org
Interactive map for state-specific information on Medicare Part D. National Mental Health Association	www.nmha.org

*The Medicare Rights Center also operates a toll-free hotline where you can get answers from counselors. Call 1-800-333-4114.

Appealing Medicare Decisions

While the federal government makes the rules about Medicare, the day-to-day administration and operation of the Medicare program are handled by private insurance companies that are contracted by the government. In the case of Medicare Part A, these insurers are called *intermediaries*, and in the case of Medicare Part B, they are referred to as *carriers*. In addition, the government contracts with committees of physicians—QIOs—to decide the appropriateness of care received by most Medicare beneficiaries who are inpatients in hospitals.

Sometimes an intermediary, carrier, or QIO will decide that a particular treatment or service is not covered by Medicare and will deny the beneficiary's claim. Many of these decisions are highly subjective and involve determining, for example, what is medically and reasonably necessary or what constitutes custodial care. If a beneficiary disagrees with a decision, there are reconsideration and appeal procedures within the Medicare program. Once Medicare's review process has been exhausted, the matter can be taken to court if the amount of money in dispute exceeds either $1,000 or $2,000, depending on the type of claim. Medicare beneficiaries can represent themselves during these appeal proceedings, or they can be represented by a personal representative or an attorney. The Medicare Rights Center estimates that only about 2 percent of Medicare beneficiaries appeal denials of care, but 80 percent of those who do appeal win more care.

Even if Medicare ultimately rejects a disputed claim, a beneficiary may not necessarily have to pay for the care he received. If a recipient did not know or could not have been expected to know that Medicare coverage would be denied for certain services, the recipient is granted a waiver of liability and the health care provider is the one who suffers the economic loss. In cases where this limited waiver of liability does not apply, however, the beneficiary is liable for any costs of care that Medicare does not cover. For example, a patient is financially responsible for any services normally provided under Medicare Part B if those services were provided by a nonparticipating provider who did not accept assignment of the claim.

Medigap Policies

With all the deductibles, copayments, and coverage exclusions, Medicare now pays for only about half of the medical costs of America's senior citizens. Much of the balance not covered by Medicare can be covered by purchasing a so-called Medigap insurance policy.

Insurance companies may only sell policies that fall into one of 12 standard benefit packages, ranging from basic coverage to the most comprehensive coverage. The 12 available Medigap policy packages are identified by the letters A through L (see chart below). Each plan package offers a different combination of benefits, allowing purchasers to choose the combination that is right for them. However, each plan package is the same across all insurance companies—thus, a C package from one insurer will be identical to a C package offered by another. Of course, the more Medigap coverage your client purchases, the more he will have to pay in premiums. All Medigap policies must provide at least the following core benefits (dollar figures are for 2008):

- $256 a day coinsurance for days 61 to 90 of a hospital stay
- $512 a day coinsurance for days 91-150 of a hospital stay (lifetime reserve days)
- All hospital approved costs from day 151 through 365

In addition, plans A through J also cover the following:

- The cost of the first three pints of blood not covered by Medicare
- The 20 percent coinsurance for Part B medical charges

Plan K offers the following benefits:

- 50 percent of the coinsurance for Part B medical services and 100 percent of preventative services
- 50 percent of the first three pints of blood
- 50 percent of hospice care cost sharing

Plan L offers the following benefits:

- 75 percent of the coinsurance for Part B medical services and 100 percent of preventative services
- 75 percent of the first three pints of blood
- 75 percent of hospice care cost sharing

The plans provide a combination of eight other areas of coverage on top of the basic set. These areas of coverage include the coinsurance for days 21 to 100 in a skilled nursing facility, the Part A and Part B deductibles, foreign travel emergencies, and prescription drug coverage.

Medigap policies do not fill all the gaps in Medicare coverage. The biggest gap they fail to bridge is for custodial care in a nursing facility or for skilled care in a nursing home beyond the first 100 days. For coverage of this type of care, one must either purchase long-term care insurance or qualify for Medicaid coverage.

Medigap policies also do not cover vision care, eyeglasses, hearing aids, or dental care unless such treatment or equipment is needed as the result of an injury. In addition, Medigap plans do not cover prescription drugs. Before January 1, 2006, prescription drugs were covered in three plan packages (plans H, I, and J). But under the Medicare Improvement

Act, which created a Medicare prescription drug program, Medigap policies offering prescription drug coverage may no longer be sold. For more on this, see the discussion on Prescription Drug Coverage above.

A 2001 report by the General Accounting Office found that it pays to shop around for a policy. Premiums vary widely not only from state to state, but within states as well. For example, researchers found that in Texas a 65-year-old consumer could pay anywhere from $300 to $1,683 for Plan A, depending on the insurer. In Ohio, plan F could range from $996 to $1,944 for an applicant of the same age.

The Center for Medicare Advocacy offers excellent on-line information about Medigap (www.medicareadvocacy.org/FAQ_Medigap.htm).

Who Should Buy Medigap Insurance?

Everyone should have one policy except for those who have other coverage or who cannot afford a Medigap policy. Many people over age 65 who are still working are covered by their employers' plans. Others may choose to receive their care from a health maintenance organization or a Medicare plan that restricts access to selected physicians. Both types of plans can take the place of Medigap insurance. If your client can qualify for Medicaid, then he does not need a Medigap policy, since Medicaid will pay for his copayments and deductibles. Despite this fact, one study found that half of Medicaid recipients pay for Medigap insurance anyway. In addition, if your client is close to being eligible for Medicaid, the state may still pay for his Medicare copayments and deductibles as well as his Part B premium under the Qualified Medicare Beneficiary program. Insurance agents who sell Medigap policies must inquire whether the potential buyer is eligible for Medicaid and whether he already has Medigap coverage. In the latter case, the agent must make a fair and accurate comparison of the existing policy and the new one the agent is offering for sale. Agents may not use high-pressure tactics and buyers have a 30-day free-look period, permitting them to return the policy for a full premium refund within that time.

How Does My Client Select a Medigap Policy?

The most important rule to follow with respect to Medigap policies is to choose only one. To purchase more than one wastes your client's premium dollar since double coverage provides no benefit except extra payments when he is ill. Since all policies must provide the same core benefits, there is much less need to compare policies to see which one provides the best coverage. Of course, your client can still compare companies for price, solvency, and customer service.

Help with Paying for Medicare

If your client does not qualify for Medicaid and cannot afford a Medigap policy, he may be able to get help paying for costs of Medicare.

There are three Medicare assistance programs, called Medicare Savings Plans:

- **Qualified Medicare Beneficiary (QMB).** The QMB program pays for Medicare Part A premiums, Medicare Part B premiums and deductibles, and coinsurance and deductibles for Part A and Part B.
- **Specified Low-income Medicare Beneficiary (SLMB).** The SLMB program pays for Medicare Part B Premiums.
- **Qualifying Individual (QI-1) Program.** The QI-1 program is an expansion of the SLMB program that one must apply for each year. It pays for Medicare's Part B Premium.

To qualify for these programs, your client must be eligible for Medicare Part A (even if he is not enrolled) and have limited income and resources. The income and resource requirements can vary from state to state, so check with your client's state before applying. In general the following limits are applied.

Personal assets, including cash, bank accounts, stocks and bonds must not exceed $4,000 for an individual and $6,000 for married couples. Your client's house and car do not count as personal assets. Some states allow additional resources above these figures; for example, New York has no resource limits for the QI-1 Program.

To apply for one of these programs, contact your state Department of Social Services office or the equivalent agency in your state.

Long-Term Care Insurance   6

If your client can afford the premiums and she is insurable, the best way to avoid or reduce significant long-term care costs is long-term care insurance. Most long-term care insurance policies today pay for home care and assisted living as well as for nursing home care. The problem lies in choosing a good policy and being able to afford it.

Long-term care insurance is a contract between an insurance company and a policyholder to pay for certain types of coverage under certain conditions. In general, long-term care policies are sold by insurance agents to policyholders, although group policies are becoming increasingly available from large employers, membership organizations like AARP, and health maintenance organizations.

The topics that we will discuss in this chapter include the following:

- Purchasing a policy
- What a good long-term care policy should include
- The tax deductibility of long-term care insurance premiums
- Advising on long-term care

Purchasing a Policy

Due to the wide range of policy options, and the lack of uniformity among policies from different companies, it can be difficult to compare long-term care policies. However, there are a few rules of thumb for purchasing a policy.

The first is to seek a qualified broker who can advise you or your clients. Also, while it's no guarantee of quality, make sure the broker has the *Certified in Long-Term Care (CLTC)* designation from the corporation for Long-Term Care Certification, Inc. (http://www.ltc-cltc.com), which provides assurance that the broker has the minimum necessary knowledge to properly advice clients.

Second, in comparing policies, ask for price quotes for policies that are similar in terms of days of coverage, amount of coverage and elimination periods. This will make them easier to compare.

Third, ask for the companies' claims history, rate of complaints, and whether they have raised premiums in the past.

Buy Enough Coverage for What You Want to Cover

How much coverage your client needs depends on her strategy. In general, she does not need to purchase a lifetime policy—three to five years worth of coverage should uually be enough. In fact, a new study from the American Association of Long-term Care Insurance shows that a three-year benefit policy is sufficient for most people. According to the study of in-force long-term care policies, only 8 percent of people needed coverage for more than three years. So, unless your client has a family history of a chronic illness, she isn't likely to need more coverage.

If your client is buying insurance as part of a Medicaid planning strategy, however, she will need to purchase at least enough insurance to cover the five-year look-back period. After moving to a nursing home or assisted living, she may want to transfer assets to her children or to whomever she would like to benefit, if she hasn't done so already. As explained in our discussion of Medicaid in Chapter 5, Medicaid penalizes such transfers by imposing a period of ineligibility that can be as long as five years (or five years for transfers to or from certain trusts). After those five years have passed, your client can qualify for Medicaid to pay her nursing home costs (provided the assets remaining in her name do not exceed Medicaid's limits).

While nursing homes are increasingly expensive, more alternatives to nursing homes exist than ever before. If your client cannot afford to purchase sufficient coverage to pay for nursing home care (including anticipated inflation), she may be able to cover the cost of home care or assisted living. In that case, you can suggest that your client think of the policy as avoiding nursing home insurance. As with other medical expenses, the inflation rate of nursing home costs is quite high. In addition, your client should probably assume that she won't be entering a nursing home for at least 10 years. By then, the cost of the nursing home will likely be twice what it is today. According to the 2006 MetLife Market Survey of Nursing Home and Home Care Costs, the average daily cost of a private room in a nursing home in the United States is $75,190 a year or $206 a day.

With those statistics in mind, here's a formula for figuring out how much coverage your client needs to purchase to cover all of the cost of nursing home care:

The average daily cost of a nursing home today times 2, minus your client's monthly income divided by 30, equals the amount of coverage to purchase.

For instance, if the average nursing home costs $206 a day and your client's monthly income is $1,500 a month, then her formula would look like this:

$$206 \times 2 = 412 - (1500/30 = 50) = 362$$

Your client should buy coverage of $362 a day. Somewhat less coverage can be purchased if your client buys an inflation rider (meaning that the insurer's payments rise with inflation) or if your client is prepared to contribute some of her savings to the cost of care.

Buy a Home Care Option or Rider

One of the problems with Medicaid is that although it pays for nursing home care, in most states it pays for only limited home care (New York State is a notable exception). Thus, people often feel financially compelled to move to a nursing home where the state will pick up the cost. Until there is a change in the law, most home care will have to be paid for out-of-pocket or by insurance. It doesn't make much sense to pay insurance premiums to replicate the Medicaid situation—coverage at a nursing home, but not at home.

Cross Your T's and Dot Your I's

Advise your client to fill out the application completely.

If your client fails to tell the insurer about an illness, the company may refuse her coverage at the time benefits are needed. It is better to be denied coverage and to be able to plan knowing that coverage is not available than it is to believe that coverage will be forthcoming, only to have it denied when it is needed. Likewise, your client should make sure that she purchases a policy from an insurance company that evaluates— or in insurance company parlance *underwrites*—the policy from day one.

If not, the company could refuse her coverage when it evaluates the application at a later date.

Compare Insurance Companies and Rates

Your client should make certain that the insurer is rated A or A+ by A. M. Best or another service that rates insurance companies. Her coverage will not be very effective if the insurer goes out of business. In addition, rates charged by insurance companies in the long-term care field tend to vary widely. Recommend to your client that she compare different companies' rates and offerings before making a decision. As we mentions above, it's important to ask for quotes on policies with similar benefits.

A Shopper's Guide to Long-Term Care Insurance

The National Association of Insurance Commissioners (NAIC) publishes *A Shopper's Guide to Long-Term Care Insurance*, a 60-page to help you and your clients determine which plan best suits their needs. For more information or to purchase the guide, visit http://www. naic.org.

Spousal Coverage

Often, a married couple will be able to afford coverage for only one spouse. Looking at statistics alone, the wife should purchase the policy. In our society, women tend to live longer than men and tend to require more care than men. The result is that women are much more likely than men to end up in a nursing home for a long period of time. In addition, the Medicaid rules provide some protection for the spouse of a nursing home resident. For these reasons, the best bet for couples who can afford the premiums for one policy only is to purchase it for the wife. Couples should bear in mind, however, that such a purchase plays the odds and is not a sure thing.

On the other hand, some companies offer incentives for both spouses to purchase coverage, either a premium discount or both spouses being able to share the same coverage.

Paying Premiums

Payment of the long-term care insurance premium should not affect one's standard of living. Thus, premiums are affordable if they are paid with money that your client would otherwise set aside to add to savings. An alternative would be for your client to purchase an annuity that pays sufficient benefits to cover the long-term care insurance premiums.

Partnership Policies

Many middle-income people have too many assets to qualify for Medicaid but can't afford a pricey long-term care insurance policy. In an effort to encourage more people to purchase long-term care insurance, the Deficit Reduction Act of 2005 (DRA) created the Qualified State Long-Term Care Partnership program. This program expands to all states the partnership programs currently available in only four states—California, Connecticut, Indiana, and New York. (A fifth state, Illinois, has a partnership program, which is technically still in effect, but few or no policies are being sold.)

The program offers special long-term care policies that allow buyers to protect assets and qualify for Medicaid when the long-term care policy runs out. Private companies sell long-term care insurance policies that have been approved by the state and meet certain standards, such as having inflation protection. The program is intended to provide incentives for people to purchase long-term care insurance policies that will cover at least some of their long-term care needs.

So far, according to the AARP, 21 additional states have enacted legislation to authorize plans under the new law. Those states are Arkansas, Colorado, Florida, Georgia, Hawaii, Idaho, Illinois, Iowa, Maryland, Massachusetts, Michigan, Missouri, Montana, Nebraska, North Dakota, Ohio, Oklahoma, Pennsylvania, Rhode Island, Virginia, and Washington.

Under the new Qualified State Long-Term Care Partnership program and California's and Connecticut's programs, the asset protection offered by partnership policies is dollar-for-dollar: For every dollar of coverage that a long-term care policy provides, its subscribers can keep a dollar in assets that normally would have to be spent down to qualify for Medicaid. So, for example, if you're client is single, she would normally be allowed only $2,000, depending on the state, in assets in order to qualify for Medicaid coverage of long-term care. But if she buys a long-term care insurance policy that provides $150,000 in benefits, she would be allowed to retain $152,000 in assets and still qualify for Medicaid. (These states set limits on the assets that can be protected.)

In New York, the partnership policy benefits are even more significant. Once a subscriber has exhausted the benefits from her long-term care partnership policy, she can qualify for Medicaid coverage no matter her level of assets. In other words, an unlimited amount of assets can be protected. However, the individual's income will be used towards her long-term care expenses.

Indiana offers each of the above models, depending on when the policy was purchased and the policy's design.

Bear in mind that currently the Medicaid asset protection will only work if your client receives her long-term care in the state where they bought the policy or in another partnership state that has a reciprocal agreement with the first state.

What a Good Long-Term Care Policy Should Include

As nursing home and long-term care costs continue to rise, the DRA has made it more difficult to qualify for Medicaid to pay for nursing home costs. Long-term care insurance can help cover expenses, but long-term care insurance contracts are notoriously confusing. How does your client figure out what is right for her? The following are some tips to help you sort through all the different options.

Coverage

Policies may cover nursing home care, home health care, assisted living, hospice care, or adult day care, or some combination of these and the more comprehensive the policy, the better. A policy that covers multiple types of care will give your client more flexibility in choosing the care that is right for her.

Waiting Period

Most long-term care insurance policies have a waiting period before benefits begin to kick in. This waiting period can be between 0 and 90 days, or even longer. Your client will have to cover all expenses during the waiting period, so she should choose a time period that she thinks she can afford to cover. A longer waiting period can mean lower premiums, but she'll need to be careful if she's getting home care. Recommend looking for a policy that bases the waiting period on calendar days. For some insurance companies, the waiting period is not based on calendar days, but is instead based on days of reimbursable service, which can be very complicated. Some policies may have different waiting periods for home health care and nursing home care, and some companies waive the waiting period for home health care altogether.

Daily Benefit

The daily benefit is the amount the insurance pays per day toward long-term care expenses. If your client's daily benefit doesn't cover her expenses, she will have to cover any additional costs. Purchasing the maximum daily benefit will ensure that your client has the most coverage available. If she wants to lower her premiums, she may consider covering a portion of the care herself. Your client can then insure for the maximum daily benefit minus the amount she is covering. The lower daily benefit will mean a lower premium.

It is important to determine how the daily benefit is calculated. It can be each day's actual charges (daily reimbursement) or the daily average calculated each month (monthly reimbursement). The latter is better for home health care because a home care worker might come for a full day one day and then only part of the day the next.

Inflation Protection

As nursing home costs continue to rise, your client's daily benefit will cover less and less of her expenses. Most insurance policies offer inflation protection of 5 percent a year, which is designed to increase the daily benefit along with the long-term care inflation rate of 5.6 percent a year. Although inflation protection can significantly increase the premium, most advisors still recommend that clients purchase it. There are two main types of inflation protection: *compound interest increases* and *simple interest increases*. If your client is purchasing a long-term care policy and is younger than age 62, she will need to purchase compound inflation protection. This can, however, more than double her premium. If she purchases a policy after age 62, some experts believe that simple inflation increases should be enough, and she will save on premium costs.

The Tax Deductibility of Long-Term Care Insurance Premiums

Qualified long-term care insurance policies receive special tax treatment. To be qualified, policies must adhere to regulations established by the National Association of Insurance Commissioners. Among the requirements are that the policy must offer the consumer the options of *inflation* and *nonforfeiture* protection, although the consumer can choose not to purchase these features.

The policies must also offer both activities of daily living (ADL) and cognitive impairment triggers, but may not offer a medical necessity trigger. *Triggers* are conditions that must be present for a policy to be activated. Under the ADL trigger, benefits may begin only when the beneficiary needs assistance with at least two of six ADLs. The ADLs are eating, toileting, transferring, bathing, dressing, or continence. In addition, a licensed health care practitioner must certify that the need for assistance with the ADLs is reasonably expected to continue for at least 90 days. Under a cognitive impairment trigger, coverage begins when the individual has been certified to require substantial supervision to protect her from threats to health and safety due to cognitive impairment.

Policies purchased before January 1, 1997, are grandfathered and treated as *qualified* as long as they have been approved by the insurance commissioner of the state in which they are sold. Most individual policies must receive approval from the insurance commission in the state in which they are sold, while most group policies do not require this approval. To determine whether a particular policy will be grandfathered, policyholders should check with their insurance broker or with their state's insurance commission.

Premiums for *qualified* long-term care policies will be treated as a medical expense and will be deductible to the extent that they, along with other un-reimbursed medical expenses (including Medigap insurance premiums), exceed 7.5 percent of the insured's adjusted gross income. If your client is self-employed, the rules are a little different. She can take the amount of the premium as a deduction as long as she made a net profit—her medical expenses do not have to exceed 7.5 percent of her income.

The deductibility of premiums is limited by the age of the taxpayer at the end of the year, as follows in Table 6.1 (the limits will be adjusted annually with inflation).

Table 6.1: Deductibility of Premiums Based on Age

Age attained before the end of the taxable year	Amount allowed as medical expenses in	
	2007	*2008*
40 or under	$ 290	$ 310
41–50	$ 550	$ 580
51–60	$1,110	$1,150
61–70	$2,950	$3,080
71 or older	$3,680	$3,850

Benefits from reimbursement policies, which pay for the actual services a beneficiary receives, are not included in income. Benefits from per diem or indemnity policies, which pay a predetermined amount each day, are not included in income except amounts that exceed the beneficiary's total qualified long-term care expenses or $270 per day (in 2008), whichever is greater.

Advising on Long-Term Care

Long-term care insurance has attracted much media attention, and many insurance agents are now selling it. However, long-term care insurance is a complex product that should be approached with caution. The authors believe that insurance agents and brokers selling long-term care insurance should be highly trained and know how to recommend the right coverage based on a client's finances and objectives.

If your client is considering long-term care insurance, you can help her determine whether she can afford this type of coverage and whether the policy she is considering meets necessary standards. You may also consider learning more about long-term care by pursuing a professional certificate in long-term care.

One professional designation is that offered by the Corporation for Long-Term Care Certification: *Certified in Long-Term Care.* The Corporation for Long-Term Care (http://www.ltc-cltc.com/) was established by a founding member of the National Academy of Elder Law Attorneys, the country's premier legal organization addressing elder law issues, and is dedicated to training agents to solve clients' long-term care needs.

Moreover, the Corporation for Long-term Care Certification program is *third* party, meaning that it is not affiliated with any insurance company or supported financially by the long-term care insurance industry. This is important because, as an agent, you would represent a number of insurance carriers so that you can help your clients choose from a variety of policies. The Corporation for Long-term Care Certification also has received the support of your state insurance regulator through the granting of continuing education credits, so it's worth investigating for a number of reasons.

Nursing Home Issues 7

Few decisions are more difficult than the one to place a spouse or parent in a nursing home. Since nursing homes are often seen as a last resort, the decision is generally overlaid by a sense of guilt. Most families try to care for loved ones at home for as long as (or longer than) possible, only accepting the inevitable when no other viable alternative is available.

In this chapter, we will discuss some of the issues you will want to keep in mind as you advise clients on nursing home-related issues such as finding a nursing home, placement, and family disputes.

The topics that we will discuss in this chapter include the following:

- Choosing and evaluating a nursing home
- Discussing placement with client families
- Resident rights
- Resolving disputes

Choosing and Evaluating a Nursing Home

Can there be a more difficult job than finding a nursing home for a parent or spouse? No one wants to live in a nursing home. They serve as institutions of last resort when it is impossible to provide the necessary care in any other setting. And, typically, the search takes place under the gun—when a hospital or rehabilitation center is threatening discharge or when it is no longer possible for a loved one to live at home. Finally, in most cases, finding the right nursing home is a once-in-a-lifetime task, one your client (or his family) is taking on without the experience of having done it before.

That said, there are a few rules of thumb that you can understand to help your clients make the right decisions.

1. **Location, location, location.** No single factor is more important to quality of care and quality of life of a nursing home resident than

visits by family members. The quality of care is often better if the facility staff knows that someone who cares is involved. Visits can be the high point of the day or week for the nursing home resident. So, advise your client to make it as easy as possible for family members and friends to visit.

2. **Get references.** Make sure your client asks the facility to provide the names of family members of residents. Then your client can ask the references about the care provided in the facility and the staff's responsiveness when the resident or his relatives raise concerns.

3. **Check certifying agency reports.** We recommend CareScout (www.carescout.com) as an unbiased source for ratings and reviews of eldercare providers nationwide. Detailed 7-10 page Nursing Home reports are available for a small fee and include over 100 pieces of information on quality, resident population profiles, and health violations.

4. **Interview the administrator and/or staff.** Your client should talk to the nursing home administrator or nursing staff about how care plans are developed for residents and how they respond to concerns expressed by family members. Your client should make sure he is comfortable with the response. It is better that he meet with and ask questions of the people responsible for care and not just the person marketing the facility.

5. **Tour the nursing home.** Advise your client to try not to be impressed by a fancy lobby or depressed by an older, more rundown facility. What matters most is the quality of care and the interactions between staff and residents. Recommend that your client see what he picks up about how well residents are attended to and whether they are treated with respect. It is also advisable to try and get a tour of the facility that is not prearranged. While this is not always possible, it does give the family members the opportunity of seeing an unrehearsed atmosphere.

Discussing Placement with Client Families

The difficulty of making the decision to place a loved one in a nursing home is compounded when family members disagree on whether the step is necessary. This is true whether the person disagreeing is the person himself who needs help, his spouse, or his child.

The placement decision can be less difficult if, to the extent possible, all family members are included in the process, including the senior in question, and if everyone is comfortable that all other options have been explored. This does not necessarily ensure unanimity in the decision, but it should help.

We recommend the following steps:

1. **Include all family members in the decision.** Advise your client that when care is needed, it is essential everyone understands what providing that care involves. Recommend that your client has family meetings, whether as a family alone or with medical and social work staff where available. If meeting together is impossible, encourage conference calls, mail, and e-mail communications—even web conferencing is a possible solution.

2. **Research other options.** Your client should find out what care can be provided at home, what kind of day care options are available outside of the home, and whether local agencies provide respite care to give the family care providers a much-needed rest. Also, recommend your client look into other residential care options, such as assisted living and congregate care facilities. Local agencies, geriatric care managers, and elder law attorneys can help answer these questions.

3. **Do the homework.** Recommend your clients follow the steps we outlined in the previous section for finding the best nursing home placement available. If your client and his family members have done the legwork, they can assuage the guilt factor at least to some extent.

4. **Hire a geriatric care manager to help in this process.** While hospitals and public agencies have social workers to help out, they are often stretched too thin to provide the level of assistance your client needs. In addition, they can have dual loyalties—to the hospital that wants a patient moved as well as to the patient. A social worker or nurse working as a private geriatric care manager can assist in finding a nursing home, investigating alternatives either at home or in another residential facility, in evaluating the senior to

determine the necessary level of care, and in communicating with family members to facilitate the decision. To find a geriatric care manager in your client's area, visit the Web site of the National Association of Professional Geriatric Care Managers at http://www.caremanager.org.

These steps cannot make the decision easy, but they can help make it less difficult for your client.

Resident Rights

While residents in nursing homes have no fewer rights than anyone else, the combination of an institutional setting and the disability that put the person in the facility in the first place often results in a loss of dignity and the absence of proper care.

As a result, in 1987, Congress enacted the Nursing Home Reform Law that has since been incorporated into the Medicare and Medicaid regulations. In its broadest terms, it requires that every nursing home resident be given whatever services are necessary to function at the highest level possible. The law gives residents a number of specific rights:

1. Residents have the right to be free of unnecessary physical or chemical restraints. Vests, hand mitts, seat belts and other physical restraints, and antipsychotic drugs, sedatives, and other chemical restraints are impermissible, except when authorized by a physician, in writing, for a specified and limited period of time.
2. To assist residents, facilities must inform them of the name, specialty, and means of contacting the physician responsible for the resident's care. Residents have the right to participate in care planning meetings.
3. When a resident experiences any deterioration in health, or when a physician wishes to change the resident's treatment, the facility must inform the resident, and the resident's physician, legal representative, or interested family member.
4. The resident has the right to gain access to all of his records within one business day and the right to access copies of those records at a cost that is reasonable in that community. The facility must explain how to examine these records or how to transfer the authority to obtain records to another person.

5. The facility must provide a written description of legal rights, explaining state laws regarding living wills, durable powers of attorney for health care and other advance directives, along with the facility's policy on carrying out these directives.

6. At the time of admission and during the stay, nursing homes must fully inform residents of the services available in the facility and of related charges. Nursing homes may charge for services and items in addition to the basic daily rate, but only if they already have disclosed what services and items will incur an additional charge and how much that charge will be.

7. The resident has a right to privacy, which is a right that extends to all aspects of care, including care for personal needs, visits with family and friends, and communication with others through telephone and mail. Residents, thus, must have areas for receiving private calls or visitors so that no one may intrude as well as to preserve the privacy of their roommates.

8. Residents have the right to share a room with a spouse, gather with other residents without staff present, and meet with state and local nursing home ombudspeople or any other agency representatives. They may leave the nursing home and belong to any church or social group. Within the home, residents have a right to manage their own financial affairs, free of any requirement that they deposit personal funds with the facility.

9. Residents also can get up and go to bed when they choose, eat a variety of snacks outside meal times, decide what to wear, choose activities, and decide how to spend their time. The nursing home must offer a choice at main meals, because individual tastes and needs vary. Residents, not staff, determine their hours of sleep and visits to the bathroom. Residents may self-administer medication.

10. Residents may bring personal possessions to the nursing home such as clothing, furnishings, and jewelry. Residents may expect staff to take responsibility for assisting in the protection of items or locating lost items and should inquire about facility policies for replacing missing items. Residents should expect kind, courteous, and professional behavior from staff. Staff should treat residents like adults.

11. Nursing home residents may not be moved to a different room, a different nursing home, a hospital, back home, or anywhere else

without advance notice, an opportunity for appeal, or a showing that such a move is in the best interest of the resident or necessary for the health of other nursing home residents.

12. The resident has a right to be free of interference, coercion, discrimination, and reprisal in exercising his rights. Being assertive and identifying problems usually brings good results, and nursing homes have a responsibility not only to assist residents in raising individual concerns, but also in responding promptly to those concerns.

Note. Nursing home residents have the right to live wherever they choose. Nursing homes that attempt to detain residents against their wishes are practicing a form of incarceration, which, of course, is illegal. On the other hand, a nursing home resident may not be able to say where he wants to live. In such cases, the matter gets murkier. If the resident's family agrees on what is best for the resident, then the family should be able to decide—not an unrelated third party. But if the nursing home attempts to fight the transfer of an incapacitated resident, the resident's family may have to set up a guardianship for the resident. Once that is done, the guardian will have the ability to decide on whether the move is appropriate or not.

Resolving Disputes

Disagreements with a nursing home can come up regarding any number of topics, and almost none are trivial because they involve the day-to-day life of the resident. Among other issues, disputes can arise about the quality of food, the level of assistance in feeding, troublesome roommates, disrespect or lack of privacy, insufficient occupational therapy, or a level and quality of activities that does not match what was promised.

The nursing homes that live up to the ideal of what your client would want for his parents or himself are few and far between. The question is how far your client can push them towards that ideal, what steps should be taken, in what process, and at what stage does the care become not only less than ideal, but so inadequate as to require legal or other intervention. This can be a hard determination to make and, in some cases, needs the involvement of a geriatric care manager who can make an independent evaluation of the resident and who has a sufficient knowledge of nursing homes to know whether the one in question is meeting the appropriate standard of care.

Exhibit 7.1 illustrates a list of the interventions your client or his family may take, in pursuing a dispute. You may want to copy this list for your clients to keep in case a dispute arises. In all cases, recommend your client take detailed notes of his contacts with facility staff. Also, recommend that he note the date and the full name of the person with whom he communicates.

Exhibit 7-1: Interventions for Resolving a Nursing Home Dispute

Use these interventions in order. Each is a strong method to gain a response from the facility:

1. Talk to staff. Let them know what you expect, what you care about, and what your family member cares about. This may easily solve the problem.
2. Talk to a supervisor, such as the nursing chief or an administrator. Explain the problem as you see it. Do so with the expectation that the issue will be favorably resolved, and it may well be.
3. Hold a meeting with the appropriate nursing home personnel. This can be a regularly scheduled care planning meeting, or you can ask for a special meeting to resolve a problem that wasn't resolved more informally.
4. Contact the ombudsperson assigned to the nursing home. He should be able to intervene and get an appropriate result. Contact information for the Ombudsman Program in your state can be found at www.ltcombudsman.org
5. If the problem constitutes a violation of the resident rights described above, report it to the state licensing agency. This should put necessary pressure on the facility.
6. Hire a geriatric care manager to intervene. An advocate for you who is not as personally involved as you and who understands how nursing homes function as institutions can help you determine what is possible to accomplish and can teach the facility to make the necessary changes.
7. Hire a lawyer. While a lawyer may be necessary to assert the resident's rights, the involvement of an attorney may also escalate the dispute to a point where it is more difficult to resolve. This is why we have listed this as the second-to-last option. But when all else fails, a lawyer has the tools to make the facility obey the law.
8. Move your relative. If nothing else works, move your family member to a better facility. This may be difficult, depending on the situation, but it may be the only solution. It does not prevent you from pursuing legal compensation for any harm inflicted on the nursing home resident while at the earlier facility.

The book, *Nursing Homes: The Family's Journey*, by Peter S. Silin, gives family members of nursing home residents important practical advice, emotional support, and explains the intricacies of care and nursing homes. It is available at http://www.nursinghomesbook.com.

Disability Planning

8

Advising clients about their options should they or a loved one become disabled is, like many elder care topics, a sensitive issue. You want to reassure your client that she does have options if faced with a life-altering disability or if her spouse or child should face one.

The topics we'll discuss in this chapter include the following:

- Supplemental security income (SSI)
- Supplemental needs trusts and planning for disabled children

Supplemental Security Income (SSI)

SSI is the basic federal safety-net program for the elderly, blind, and disabled, providing them with a minimum guaranteed income. Effective January 1, 2008, the maximum federal SSI benefit is $637 a month for an individual and $956 a month for a couple (the amounts go up every January 1). These amounts are supplemented in most states.

Although the Social Security Administration (SSA) administers the program, eligibility for SSI benefits is based on financial need alone, not on how long a client has worked or how much she has paid into Social Security. However, the financial eligibility rules are quite stringent.

About 6.6 million persons were receiving SSI payments in December 2000. Fifty-seven percent of these recipients were between the ages of 18 and 64, 30 percent were aged 65 or older, and 13 percent were under age 18. Many older persons who are not eligible for Social Security retirement benefits (because they have not accumulated enough work credits) may nevertheless be eligible for SSI, and many of those receiving Social Security may be able to supplement their benefits with SSI payments. It is estimated that 1.5 million elderly who are potentially eligible for benefits never apply for them.

SSI Benefits

Most states supplement the federal SSI payment with payments of their own. The states that do not pay a supplement are Arkansas, Georgia, Kansas, Mississippi, Tennessee, Texas, and West Virginia. In some states that do pay a supplement, a client may qualify for the state payment even if she doesn't meet the federal SSI eligibility criteria. But even in those states that do supplement the federal payment, the total SSI benefit usually falls below the poverty level. (For more information on state supplements, visit the SSA Web site, http://www.ssa.gov.)

The idea of the SSI program is to provide a floor income level. If your client is receiving income from another source, her SSI benefit will be cut dollar for dollar. In addition, the SSA deems the food and shelter the applicant receives from another source to be *in kind* income. As a result, actual payment amounts vary depending on her income, living arrangements, and other factors.

While the SSI program's benefits are meager, in most states, SSI recipients are also automatically eligible to receive Medicaid, which can pay for hospital stays, doctor bills, prescription drugs, nursing home care, and other health costs. SSI recipients may also be eligible for food stamps in every state except California and, in some cases, for special programs for the developmentally delayed.

Who Is Eligible for SSI?

To be eligible for SSI, a client

- Must be either age 65 or older, blind, or disabled
- Must be a citizen of the U.S. or be a long-time resident who meets certain strict requirements
- Must have a monthly income of less than a minimum threshold established by her state
- Must have less than $2,000 in assets ($3,000 for a couple), although certain resources are excluded in the eligibility determination (see the following section, "Income Limits")

Income Limits

The amount of income a client can earn and still qualify for SSI differs from state to state. (To find out income limits, call toll free 1-800-772-1213 or check with the local SSA office.) In many states, the income limit for eligibility is the same as the maximum federal benefit—$637 a month for an individual and $956 for couples in 2008. If a client's income falls below these thresholds, she is eligible for benefits. The benefit will be the difference between the client's income and the SSI benefit in her state. For instance, if her income is $400 a month, and the SSI benefit for a single individual in the applicant's state is $600 a month, the applicant will receive an SSI check of $200 a month.

At some level, it may not seem worth the trouble to apply and stay eligible for SSI, but as it is mentioned above, the ancillary benefits—especially Medicaid—may make it worthwhile to maintain SSI even if the financial payment is only a few dollars a month. Certain sources of income and support are *not counted* in determining eligibility, and what may appear to you to be income may not be counted as such by the local Social Security or welfare office. Therefore, if the applicant is living on a small fixed income and has few resources or assets, it is worth her while to apply for benefits.

In determining whether a client's income is low enough to qualify her for benefits, the SSA counts the money she earns in wages or from self-employment, as well as any investment income, pensions, annuities, gifts (except gifts of clothing), rents, and interest. Social Security and Veterans benefits are also considered income. Free housing received from friends or relatives may be counted as income as well, based on what such housing would cost in the applicant's area.

However, in totaling the applicant's income, the SSA *does not* count the following:

- The first $20 per month she receives from most income
- The first $65 a month she earns from wages or self-employment, and only half of the amount she earns above $65
- Irregular earned or unearned income of not more than $10 and $20 a month, respectively
- Food stamps, home energy assistance, and most food, clothing, or shelter received from non-profit organizations

Resource Limits

As noted above, the applicant can have no more than $2,000 in countable resources ($3,000 for a married couple living together) to be eligible for SSI. Countable resources or assets include bank accounts, investments, real estate (other than the applicant's residence), and personal property. Also included is any money or property that a client holds jointly with someone else. (The SSA determines how much a client's partial ownership is worth and counts that as a resource.)

However, certain property of value is *not* counted in determining eligibility for SSI, including the following belonging to the applicant:

- Her home and the land it is on, no matter how valuable it is
- Personal and household goods
- A car (only one) of any value if it is used for transportation for the applicant or a member of her household
- Wedding and engagement rings
- Property for self-support, such as tools, up to $6,000 in value
- Burial plots
- Life insurance and burial funds up to $1,500 for each person

Transferring Resources to Qualify for SSI

If a client's resources are still above these limits, she may be able to *spend down* to qualify for SSI, similar to the process to qualify for the Medicaid program. After she applies for benefits, she has a certain time period—six months for real estate and three months for personal property and liquid assets—to sell or spend her excess resources for fair market value to come under the benefit limits.

If she gives away a resource or sells it for less than it is worth in order to get under the SSI resource limit, she may be ineligible for SSI for up to 36 months. The SSA looks at whether or not your client has transferred a resource within the previous three years. If she has, it computes a penalty period by dividing the amount of the transfer by her monthly benefit amount.

Thus, if your client gives her son a $6,000 gift and then applies for a monthly SSI benefit of $600 within three years of the gift, she will not be eligible for SSI for ten months (6,000/600 = 10). That ten-month period will begin on the date of the transfer and end ten months later. In other words, although she can be ineligible for up to 36 months due to a transfer, that is only a cap. The actual period of ineligibility is based on the value of what you transferred divided by the monthly benefit in the applicant's state.

Clients should be aware that transfers may be cured by the gift recipient returning the gift to a client. And, finally, there are certain exceptions to the transfer penalty. These include gifts to

- A spouse (or anyone else for the spouse's benefit)
- A blind or disabled child
- A trust for the benefit of a blind or disabled child
- Life insurance and burial funds up to $1,500 for each person
- A trust for the sole benefit of a disabled individual under age 65 (even if the trust is for the benefit of the applicant, under certain circumstances)

In addition, special exceptions apply to the transfer of a home. The SSI applicant may freely transfer her home to the following individuals without incurring a transfer penalty:

- The applicant's spouse
- A child who is under age 21 or who is blind or disabled
- Into a trust for the sole benefit of a disabled individual under age 65 (even if the trust is for the benefit of the applicant, under certain circumstances)
- A sibling who has lived in the home during the year preceding the applicant's institutionalization and who already holds an equity interest in the home
- A *caretaker child*, who is defined as a child of the applicant who lived in the house for at least two years prior to the applicant's institutionalization and who during that period provided care that allowed the applicant to avoid a nursing home stay

Trusts

The contents of most trusts your client creates for herself will be considered available to her in determining her eligibility for SSI. On the other hand, assets of most trusts that someone else creates and names your client a beneficiary of will not be considered to belong to your client for purposes of determining her SSI eligibility.

When Congress created the rules limiting trusts for SSI purposes, it created a *safe harbor*, which permits your client to place money into two types of trusts for her own benefit. In doing so, it adopted safe harbors already created for Medicaid purposes. The safe harbors apply to supplemental needs trusts established by a parent, grandparent, guardian or court solely for the benefit of a disabled person under age 65, *pooled trusts* established by non-profit associations under Section 1917(d)(4)(c) of the Social Security Act, and Miller Trusts established in *income-cap* states under Section 1917 (d)(4)(B) of the Social Security Act.

Given the complexity of this field, any trust should be drafted by an experienced attorney knowledgeable about SSI matters.

How to Apply for SSI Benefits

If you think your client qualifies for SSI benefits, recommend that she call or visit her local SSA office and apply. (For on-line help in finding your local SSA office, visit http://www.ssa.gov.) If an applicant's state offers payments supplementing the federal SSI benefit, she may have to apply for that supplement at her local county social welfare office. Some have the federal government administer their supplements, while other states administer the supplements themselves. In these latter states, application for the supplement must be made separately with the state agency. For a listing of states with federally administered supplements, visit http://www.ssa.gov.

An applicant needs to provide the SSA with proof of age and citizenship or legal residence, as well as provide detailed information about her financial situation. Usually, an SSA claims representative interviews the applicant and completes the forms using the information she supplies.

An applicant should apply as soon as possible so that she does not lose benefits. If she calls SSA to make an appointment to apply, SSA will use the date of her call as her application filing date.

If her application is denied, an applicant can appeal. The appeals process is similar to that for appealing Social Security claims denials.

Once an individual begins receiving benefits, the SSA reviews will review her SSI eligibility once every one to three years.

Supplemental Needs Trusts and Planning for Disabled Children

Americans are living longer than they did in years past, including those with disabilities. According to one count, 480,000 adults with mental retardation are living with parents who are 60 years-old or older. This figure does not include adult children with other forms of disability nor does it include those who live separately, but still depend on their parents for vital support.

When these parents can no longer care for their children due to their own disability or death, the responsibility often falls on siblings, other family members, and the community. In many cases, expenses will increase dramatically when care and guidance provided by parents must instead be provided by a professional for a fee.

Planning by parents can make all the difference in the life of the child with a disability, as well as that of her siblings who may be left with the responsibility for caretaking (on top of their own careers and caring for their own families and, possibly, ailing parents). Any plan should include the following elements:

- A plan of care
- Supplemental needs trust
- Life insurance

Let's discuss these three areas in more detail.

A Plan of Care

Where will a child live when she can no longer live with her parents? Will she move in with a sibling? Or into a group home? Who will make the decision? Who will monitor the care she receives? It's never too soon to begin answering these questions and making sure that living and support arrangements are in place.

In some cases, it can ease the transition for all of those concerned if the child moves to the new living arrangement while her parents can still help with the process. In many parts of the country, non-profit organizations and private consultants can help set up the plan, research available options, and assist in the move.

It will help everyone involved if the parents create a written statement of their wishes for their child's care. They know her better than anyone else. They can explain what helps, what hurts, what scares their child (who, of course, is an adult), and what reassures her. When the parents are gone, their knowledge will go with them unless they pass it on.

In almost all cases where a parent will leave funds upon her death to a disabled child, it should be done in the form of a trust. Trusts set up for the care of a disabled child generally are called *supplemental* or *special needs* trusts, which are described in more detail below.

Money should not go outright to the child, both because she may not be able to manage it properly and because receiving the funds directly may cause the child to lose public benefits, such as Supplemental Security Income (SSI) and Medicaid. Often, these programs also serve as the entry point for receiving vital community support services.

Some parents choose to avoid the complication of a trust by leaving their estates to one or more of their healthy children, relying on them to use the funds for the benefit of their disabled siblings. Except in the case of a very small estate, this is generally not a good idea. It puts the healthy child in the difficult position of having to decide how much of her money to spend on her sibling. Such funds also will be subject to claim by creditors and at risk in the event of divorce or bankruptcy. Finally, the child who receives the funds may die before the disabled child without setting these funds aside in her estate plan.

Supplemental Needs Trusts

Supplemental needs trusts (also known as special needs trusts) allow a disabled beneficiary to receive gifts, lawsuit settlements, or other funds without losing her eligibility for certain government programs. Such trusts are drafted so that the funds will not be considered to belong to the beneficiary in determining her eligibility for public benefits. As their name implies, supplemental needs trusts are designed not to provide basic support, but instead to pay for comforts and luxuries that are not available from public assistance funds. These trusts typically pay for things like education, recreation, counseling, and medical attention beyond the simple necessities of life. (However, the trustee can use trust funds for food, clothing, and shelter—despite a possible loss or reduction in public assistance—if the trustee decides doing so is in the beneficiary's best interest.)

Very often, supplemental needs trusts are created by a parent or other family member for a disabled child (even though the child may be an adult by the time the trust is created or funded). Such trusts also may be set up in a will as a way for an individual to leave assets to a disabled relative. In addition, the disabled individual can often create the trust herself, depending on the program for which she seeks benefits. These *self-settled* trusts are frequently established by individuals who become disabled as the result of an accident or medical malpractice and later receive the proceeds of a personal injury award or settlement.

Each public benefits program has restrictions that the supplemental needs trust must comply with in order not to jeopardize the beneficiary's continued eligibility for public benefits. Both Medicaid and SSI are quite restrictive, making it difficult for a beneficiary to create a trust for her own benefit and still retain eligibility for Medicaid benefits. But both programs allow two safe harbors, permitting the creation of supplemental needs trusts with a beneficiary's own money if the trust meets certain requirements.

The first of these is called a *payback* or *(d)(4)(A) trust*, referring to the authorizing statute. Payback trusts are created with the assets of a disabled individual under age 65 and are established by her parent, grandparent, or legal guardian or by a court. The trust also must provide that at the beneficiary's death any remaining trust funds will first be used to reimburse the state for Medicaid paid on the beneficiary's behalf.

Medicaid and SSI law also permits *(d)(4)(c)* or *pooled trusts*. Such trusts pool the resources of many disabled beneficiaries, and those resources are managed by a non-profit association. Unlike individual disability trusts, which may be created only for those under age 65, pooled trusts may be created for beneficiaries of any age and may be created by the beneficiary herself. In addition, upon the beneficiary's death, the state does not have to be repaid for its Medicaid expenses on her behalf as long as the funds are retained in the trust for the benefit of other disabled beneficiaries. (At least, that's what the federal law says . . . some states require reimbursement under all circumstances.) Although a pooled trust is an option for a disabled individual over age 65 who is receiving Medicaid or SSI, those over age 65 who make transfers to the trust will incur a transfer penalty. (For more information about the transfer penalty, see Chapter 4, "Medicaid and Medicaid Planning.")

Income paid from a supplemental needs trust to a beneficiary is another issue, particularly with regard to SSI benefits. In the case of SSI, the trust beneficiary would lose a dollar of SSI benefits for every dollar paid directly to her. In addition, payments by the trust to the beneficiary for food, clothing, or housing are considered *in kind* income and, again, the SSI benefit will be cut dollar for dollar. Some attorneys draft the trusts to limit the trustee's discretion to make such payments. Others do not limit the trustee's discretion, but instead counsel the trustee on how the trust funds may be spent, permitting more flexibility for unforeseen events or changes in circumstances in the future. The difference has to do with philosophy, the situation of the client, and the amount of money in the trust.

Choosing a trustee is also an important issue in supplemental needs trusts. Most people do not have the expertise to manage a trust. An alternative is retaining the services of a professional trustee. For those who may be uncomfortable with the idea of an outsider managing a loved one's affairs, it is possible to simultaneously appoint a *trust protector*, who has the powers to review accounts and to hire and fire trustees, and a trust *advisor*, who can instruct the trustee on the beneficiary's needs. However, if the trust fund is small, a professional trustee may not be interested. Such a problem can be an argument for pooled trusts.

Life Insurance

A parent with a disabled child should consider buying life insurance to fund the supplemental needs trust set up for the child's support. What may look like a substantial sum to leave in trust today may run out after several years of paying for care that the parent had previously provided. The more resources available, the better the support provided to the child. And if both parents are alive, the cost of "second-to-die" insurance—payable only when the second of the two parents passes away—can be surprisingly low. The good news is that advance planning for a disabled child can make a significant difference in the child's life. You just have to take the first step.

For more information on special needs planning, go to http://www. specialneedsanswers.com or consult with an elderlaw attorney or a member of the Academy of Special Needs Planners, the organization of attorneys that created and host the website.

Retirement Living

9

Studies show that, if they possibly can, older Americans prefer to stay in their own homes. It is no surprise, then, that most care of the elderly is provided at home, either by family or by hired help. While many consider in-home care preferable to institutional care, there are public benefits and legal considerations that come into play as well.

State and federal government officials are slowly recognizing that home care can be more cost-effective than institutional care. This means that, depending on the state, financial or other assistance may be available for those who choose to remain in their homes despite declining capabilities.

In this chapter, we will discuss some issues of home care and alternatives for out-of-home care.

The topics covered in this chapter include the following:

- Remaining in the home
- Obtaining outside help
- Respite services
- Low-income housing for seniors
- Alternatives to nursing homes

Remaining in the Home

Family members shoulder most of the burden of caring for the elderly at home. Being the primary caretaker for someone who requires assistance with activities of daily living, such as walking, eating, and toileting can be a consuming and sometimes exhausting task. One important consideration when one family member bears the sole responsibility of caring for a parent or other older relative is the question of equity with other family members. For example, is the family member being fairly compensated for his work? If the older person is living with a child, does the parent contribute towards the home expenses? If the care is taking place in the elder's home, does the child have an ownership interest in the house?

For a parent with only one child, such arrangements may not be so complicated, but if the parent has more than one child, it can be difficult to know what is fair. An arrangement that seems equitable today may not seem that way after a child has devoted, for example, five years to the care of the parent. And if a plan is set up that is fair for five years of care, what happens if the parent suddenly moves into a nursing home during the first year? With no planning for such eventualities, the care of an older person can foster resentment and guilt among siblings and family members. As an adviser, you can help families devise creative solutions to such problems.

Getting Outside Help

Public and private agencies offer a variety of home care services that may be available to your client and include the following services:

- Home health care, either part-time or 24-hour care
- Personal care and homemaking services, such as shopping, cooking, and cleaning
- Services delivered to the home, such as meal programs, transportation, and home repair
- Adult day care centers that offer more intensive services than senior centers (There are more than 2,000 such centers around the nation that are usually affiliated with churches or non-profit community agencies.)
- Money management
- Respite services (These programs provide caretakers with a periodic break. A home care professional or aide substitutes for the caretaker for a specified period of time.)

Medicare and Medicaid provide some coverage of the medical portion of home health care. Although the coverage is often inadequate, when combined with other resources available to the client and his family, it may be enough to keep a fragile older person at home for a longer period of time. Medicaid offers very little in the way of home care except in New

York State, which provides home care to all Medicaid recipients who need it. Recognizing that home care can cost far less than nursing home care, a few other states—notably Hawaii, Oregon, and Wisconsin—are pioneering efforts to provide services to those who remain in their homes.

Utilizing Monthly Social Security and Retirement Checks for Family Providing Care

Most care provided to seniors and others with disabilities is provided by family members. There is nothing wrong with compensating those family members, as long as everyone agrees. To make sure there are no misunderstandings, it is best that such agreements be put in writing. Otherwise, years from now, those involved in the care may have different memories of what the arrangement was. Also, money received for the care of someone else should be reported as taxable income.

There are thousands of private home care agencies around the nation. About half of these are Medicare or Medicaid Certified Home Care Agencies, meaning that these two federal programs will reimburse for services provided by the agency if the services are covered. Such certification also means that the agency has met certain minimum federal standards regarding patient care and finances. Home care agencies can also gain accreditation from private accrediting organizations. The three major accrediting groups for home care agencies are the Community Health Accreditation Program (http://www.chapinc.org); the Joint Commission on Accreditation of Healthcare Organizations (http://www.jcaho.org); and the National Association for Home Care (http://www.nahc.org).

Non-medical services are also available to help older persons remain independent. The Older Americans Act funds more than 10,000 senior centers and gives grants to State and Area Agencies on Aging to provide services to seniors that include Meals-on-Wheels, transportation, respite care, housekeeping and personal care, money management, and shopping. Services are usually free but staffing may be limited. To find Area Agencies on Aging programs across the country, visit the Eldercare Locator Web site at http://www.eldercare.gov or call the nationwide, toll free Eldercare Locator at 1-800-677-1116. In many cases, these agencies may offer case management and coordination services as well.

The new profession of private geriatric care manager has evolved to help coordinate services for seniors. Private geriatric care managers usually have a background in either social work, nursing, or psychology and are experts in helping older persons and their families make arrangements for various kinds of long-term health care. These care managers evaluate an older person's needs, review the options available, and monitor care once it is being delivered. To find a geriatric care manager in your area, visit the Web site of the National Association of Professional Geriatric Care Managers at http://www.caremanager.org.

Respite Services

Caring for a loved one with a long-term illness is more than a full-time job. Caregivers need occasional time away from their responsibilities to rejuvenate, pursue personal interests, or socialize. Respite services give caregivers that opportunity.

There are many different types of respite services, including the following:

- **Round-the-clock.** Assisted living facilities and nursing homes may provide overnight, weekend, and longer respite services for caregivers who need an extended period of time off. Not all assisted living facilities and nursing homes accept people for short-term stays, however.
- **Adult day care.** If a caregiver works, an adult day care facility can help. Adult day care facilities provide care and companionship outside of the home and give seniors the chance to interact with peers. The facility can provide social or therapeutic activities. Some day care facilities are especially designed for Alzheimer's patients.
- **In-home care.** If your client doesn't want to leave home, he can take advantage of one of the many in-home services that may be available. In-home care can involve a large range of services, including companionship services to help entertain loved ones, services to help the caregiver do housekeeping chores, personal care services, and skilled or medical care services, or both. In addition, your client can have someone come in to stay with his loved one while he works or for longer periods when he needs to be out of town.

The cost of respite services varies from service to service. Medicare does not pay for these services, but Medicaid may pay for adult day care services. There may be other federal or state aid available. Your client can contact the local Area Agency on Aging at http://www.aoa.gov for more information.

To find respite services, go to http://www.respitelocator.org. If your client is caring for an Alzheimer's patient, his local Alzheimer's foundation (which he can find through http://www.alz.org) may have support groups and other help for caregivers.

Low-Income Housing for Seniors

Seniors who cannot afford a private retirement home may be able to qualify for federal or state funded low-income housing. Both the federal and state governments have specific housing programs for seniors. Seniors can also apply for regular multi-family government-funded housing.

There are two types of government-funded housing: public and subsidized. Public housing is housing owned by a housing authority, and the housing authority acts as landlord. Once your client applies and is admitted to public housing, he receives an apartment. Subsidized housing is housing owned by a private landlord who receives subsidies in exchange for renting to low-income seniors. Some subsidized housing is similar to public housing—once your client is admitted, he gets an apartment—but with some types of subsidized housing, once the client applies and is admitted, he receives a rental voucher and has to find his own apartment.

In both programs, rent is calculated as a percentage of your client's income. The exact percentage varies from program to program and state to state, but it is usually around 30 percent or 40 percent.

Each program has different eligibility requirements, and the exact requirements vary from state to state. In general, the criteria for eligibility are an individual's age, household size, income level, and immigration status:

- **Age.** To be eligible for federally funded public housing, the head of household or a spouse must be at least 62 years of age. State funded programs may have different age limits. As long as the head of household meets the age requirement, your client may have younger individuals living with him.

- **Household size.** The number of people in your client's household must be able to fit into the apartment, and senior housing usually consists of studios or one-bedroom apartments. Your client is allowed to have a live-in aide as part of the household.
- **Income.** Your client's household's yearly income must be below a certain average income for the area, called the *area median income*. This amount changes every year, and it depends on family size and the area where the development is located. To see the income limits for your client's area, go to http://www.huduser.org/datasets/il.html.
- **Immigration status.** Federal housing requires that at least one member of the household be a U.S. citizen or have a certain type of legal immigration status.

To apply, your client needs to request an application from each housing authority or program to which he wishes to apply. For information on what housing is available in your client's state, go to http://www.hud.gov/groups/seniors.cfm.

Unfortunately, there are often more applicants than available housing. As a result, housing authorities and landlords keep applicants on waiting lists. These waiting lists can be quite long. Because of the wait, it is important for your client to apply to as many different housing programs as he can, to keep track of his applications, and to monitor his place on the waiting lists. Also, if he moves, advise him to be sure to notify the places where he submitted applications.

Certain applicants may be able to get a preference or priority status on the waiting list. The particular preferences and priorities vary from program to program, but common ones include the following:

- Local residents
- People facing domestic violence
- Working people (This preference must always include people who cannot work due to disability or age.)
- People who are homeless or at risk
- People with disabilities
- Veterans
- Elderly or near-elderly

If your client fits into a preference or a priority, he may be moved up the waiting list.

Once your client reaches the top of the waiting list, the housing authority or landlord will determine whether he is income eligible. Then they will check certain information, such as credit reports, criminal record information, and landlord references, to determine if your client is likely to be a good tenant. Once that is completed, he can move in.

Alternatives to Nursing Homes

The reality is that it is sometimes impossible or too expensive for an elderly person in poor health to remain at home. Other seniors may simply wish to live with others rather than be isolated. Fortunately, over the last two decades there has been an explosion of supportive housing alternatives for seniors, and the options are no longer limited to an agonizing choice between staying at home and moving to a nursing home. If your client (or his loved one) does not require round-the-clock skilled nursing care, one of these supportive housing alternatives may be just right.

Supportive housing options range from board and care homes to large institutional complexes. Supportive facilities provide food, shelter, and personal assistance while encouraging independence and personal dignity. The services offered may include help with activities such as eating, dressing, preparing meals, shopping, as well as monitoring and other supervision.

National Center on Assisted Living's Annual Reference List

The National Center on Assisted Living compiles an annual list of state regulations that includes contact information for licensing agencies. While helpful for beginning research, it does not include citations or listings of resident rights. For more information, visit http://www.ncal.org/.

The main alternatives are board and care facilities, assisted living facilities, and continuing care retirement communities (CCRCs). But these broad categories encompass a huge range of options in terms of services and costs. Generally, the more your client pays, the more services he (or his loved one) will receive. There is a great disparity in quality as well, with facilities ranging from excellent to sub-standard. This means your client needs to research the options carefully before making a choice, and by reading this next section, you can help in that process.

Board and Care Facilities

Board and care facilities are group residences that can range in size from as few as two residents to more than 200. They may also be referred to as residential care facilities, homes for the aged, or community-based residential facilities. Such facilities provide room, board, and 24-hour supervision, as well as help with the five activities of daily living (eating, dressing, bathing, using a toilet, and transferring from one position to another) and the instrumental activities of daily living (preparing meals, walking outdoors, taking medications, shopping, housekeeping, using the telephone, and handling money).

Such facilities generally do not provide any medical services. These homes may be unlicensed, and even licensed homes may rarely be monitored by the state. Costs can range from $350 to $3,000 a month. For those with very limited incomes, Supplemental Security Income may help pay the cost of these homes. Medicaid may also reimburse the monthly fee, depending on the state and the resident's Medicaid eligibility.

Assisted Living Facilities

Assisted living facilities offer basically the same services as board and care homes, but in a more upscale and homelike environment. Housing is often in small apartments and there is generally more space, privacy, and recreational options. A premium is placed on retaining as much independence in living as possible, and care is more individualized. Despite the emphasis on independence, supportive services are available 24 hours a day in order to provide different levels of help with activities of daily living. There also may be more medical supervision than is available in a board and care home, depending on the facility.

While costlier than board and care facilities, assisted living facilities nevertheless are often less expensive than nursing homes. Assisted living facility residents agree to pay a monthly rent, which can range from less than $1,000 to $6,000 a month. According to a 2005 MetLife survey, the average cost of an assisted living facility in the U.S. is $2,905 a month, or $34,860 a year. The highest average monthly cost was in Boston, Massachusetts, at $4,629, while the lowest was in Jackson, Mississippi, at $1,642.

This rent may cover all services or there may be charges for services above the monthly fee on a per-use basis. Residents generally pay the cost of medical care from their own financial resources. Some costs may be reimbursed by an individual's health insurance program or long-term care insurance policy. Because assisted living facilities are usually less expensive than nursing homes, many state Medicaid programs now provide some type of funding for elderly residents who qualify for the Medicaid program.

However, assisted living facilities are an emerging industry and not all states regulate such centers to protect residents from substandard care or questionable business practices. The National Center on Assisted Living (http://www.ncal.org) compiles an annual list of state regulations that includes contact information for licensing agencies.

To download (in PDF format) a Government Accountability Office report, "Assisted Living: Examples of State Efforts to Improve Consumer Protections" (GAO-04-684, April 30, 2004), visit http://www.gao.gov.

For names of assisted living facilities near you, the following are several helpful sites: Senior Housing Net (http://www.seniorhousingnet.com), Your Senior Resource Guide (http://www.yoursrg.com), and ElderCarelink (http://www.eldercarelink.com).

Fighting an Assisted Living Discharge

When your client moves into an assisted living complex, he expects to spend the rest of his days there. However, many assisted living residents suddenly find themselves facing eviction from their homes when their health deteriorates. Although there is no one-size-fits-all way to handle a discharge from a facility, there are some things you can try.

In general, assisted living facilities have a lot of discretion to determine when to discharge a resident. According to the National Senior Citizens Law Center, 39 states allow a facility to discharge a patient if the facility can no longer meet the patient's needs. The other 11 states (Connecticut, Georgia, Kentucky, Maryland, Massachusetts, Minnesota, Nebraska, New Hampshire, New Jersey, North Dakota, and Rhode Island) are either silent about discharge or provide other reasons for discharge, such as the resident requiring services that exceed the facility's license or the resident violating the admission agreement.

Almost all states require facilities to give residents notice of discharge, but the rules vary widely from state to state. In addition, laws regulating assisted living facilities are vague. While this gives facilities a lot of discretion, your client can also use it to his advantage.

If your client is facing a discharge that he does not believe is fair, he should remain in the facility, if possible. In a few states (Massachusetts, New York, and Iowa), assisted living discharge is considered an eviction and is handled under landlord-tenant law. That means the facility is required to go to court before it can evict a patient, where your client can get a chance to argue against the eviction. In other states, whether an assisted living discharge is regarded as an eviction is an open question. Because the rules are vague, the facility may not know what to do if your client does not leave, and by staying, he can change the balance of power. The facility would likely be forced to get a court order to move him out, and he may be able to argue that the discharge is unfair.

Some states may have procedures by which your client can object to the discharge. The procedures vary from state to state. Your client may be able to meet with a staff member or an administrator who made the discharge decision or file a complaint with the state licensing board. In a few states (Maine, Ohio, Oklahoma, Oregon, Vermont, and Wisconsin), your client has the right to an administrative hearing.

If all else fails, your client may be able to use anti-discrimination laws to challenge the discharge. The Americans with Disabilities Act, the Fair Housing Amendments Act of 1988, and Section 504 of the Rehabilitation Act all protect tenants against discrimination on the basis of a physical or mental disability. Landlords are required to reasonably accommodate a disability unless it would cause an undue hardship. So, for example, if the reason your client is being discharged is because he is now in a wheelchair and his assisted living apartment does not have ramps, he may be able to argue that the landlord is required to install the ramps as a reasonable accommodation.

Note: Using anti-discrimination law is very difficult and would require the assistance of a lawyer.

Continuing Care Retirement Communities (CCRCs)

Continuing care retirement communities (CCRCs) offer the entire residential continuum—from independent housing to assisted living to round-the-clock nursing services—under one roof. Residents pay an entry fee and an adjustable monthly rent in return for the guarantee of care for the rest of their life. Because CCRCs maintain an assortment of on-site medical and social services and facilities, residents can enter the community while still relatively healthy and then move on to more intensive care as it becomes necessary. Nursing care is often located within the CCRC or at a related facility nearby. In addition to health care services, CCRCs also typically provide meals, housekeeping, maintenance, transportation, social activities, and security. Communities range in size from about 100 to 500 living units

CCRCs are so diverse in their offerings and personality that the saying in the industry is that "if you've seen one CCRC, you've seen one CCRC." The physical plants of CCRCs run the gamut from urban highrises to garden apartments, cottages, cluster homes, or single-family homes. Some CCRCs provide units that are designed for people with special medical conditions, such as Alzheimer's disease.

Most importantly, CCRCs guarantee a life-long place to live. Assisted living and even skilled nursing facilities make no such guarantees, and, in fact, they may ask residents to leave if they believe they cannot provide the care required. However, virtually no CCRC will guarantee an individual entry into the skilled nursing facility that is a part of the CCRC. If all the nursing units are filled (by either other residents or non-residents), the CCRC may place the ailing resident in another nursing home in the community.

The downside of CCRCs is the cost, which can be greater than what people with low or moderate income and assets can afford. Prices depend on the amount of care provided, the type of contract, and the unit's size and geographic location. Entry fees run from $20,000 to more than $500,000, with monthly charges ranging from $200 to $3,200. Often seniors use the proceeds from the sale of their homes to make the initial investment in the retirement community. However, the Internal Revenue Service does not allow home sellers to roll over their capital gains into the purchase of a CCRC unit. Thus, a tax may be due on gains from the sale of a home even though a CCRC unit is being purchased with the proceeds.

Your client may be entitled to a refund of his entry fee on a declining scale if the refund is requested within a short time after moving in. Generally a refund will no longer be available after a specified period of residency. Some refundable fees revert to his estate when his unit is sold, while others do not.

CCRC Fee Arrangements

Although the entry and monthly fee arrangement is the most common, some CCRCs offer rental or equity arrangements. Under a rental arrangement, residents pay only a monthly fee, which typically covers housing and designated services (sometimes including health care services). Under equity arrangements, residents purchase their residence in the same way they would purchase a cooperative apartment or condominium, although the resale of the unit is usually limited to those who meet the community's eligibility criteria. Residents then may purchase service and health care packages for an additional fee.

CCRCs often allow your client to choose from three different fee schedules:

1. **Extensive contracts.** These include unlimited long-term nursing care at little or no increase in the monthly fee. This arrangement requires residents to pay a higher fee initially.
2. **Modified contracts.** These include a specified duration of long-term nursing care, beyond which fees rise as care increases.
3. **Fee-for-service contracts.** These exist when residents pay a reduced monthly fee but pay full daily rates for long-term nursing care.

As with assisted living facilities, the regulation of CCRCs is spotty. These institutions are strictly regulated in some states, while not at all in others, and there is no overarching federal agency that watchdogs retirement communities. A private non-profit organization, the Commission on Accreditation of Rehabilitation Facilities (CARF), accredits CCRCs. The CARF accreditation process is voluntary. Its high cost and the length of time it takes to complete the process means that accreditation is a good indicator of a facility's quality. The CARF's Web site lists all CCRCs that have been accredited. Go to http://www.carf.org/.

A CCRC's lack of accreditation should not necessarily be taken as a bad sign. One of the most important considerations is the financial soundness of the facility. In selecting a community, experts recommend choosing a *mature* facility, one that has been in business a number of years. In addition, it is important to know who the CCRC's sponsor is. The Society of Friends (Quakers), for example, has been in the CCRC business for quite some time and its facilities are reputed to be excellent. The *American Association of Homes and Services for the Aging* is the national association for non-profit CCRCs (most CCRCs are operated by non-profit groups). The group's Web site, http://www.aahsa.org, includes tips on selecting a CCRC.

CCRC Entry Requirements

Most CCRCs require that a resident be in good health, be able to live independently and be within minimum and maximum age limits when entering the facility. As a prerequisite to admission, facilities may also require both Medicare Part A and Part B, and perhaps Medigap coverage as well. A few are now even requiring long-term care coverage as a way of keeping fees down. Some CCRCs are affiliated with a specific religious, ethnic, or fraternal order and membership in these groups may be a requirement. Of course, applicants will have to demonstrate that they have the means to meet the required fees. Your client may be placed on a waiting list, because CCRCs are often sought after.

CCRC residents usually fund their care out of their own pockets. However, Medicare, and at times Medicaid, can be used to pay for certain services, and most CCRCs accept either Medicare or Medicaid. Although Medicare does not generally cover long-term nursing care, it often covers specific services that a CCRC resident might receive, such as physician services and hospitalization. Because the financial requirements for residence are fairly strict and the costs are relatively high, very few CCRC residents are eligible for Medicaid.

Evaluating a Facility and Contract

Deciding on a CCRC is a once-in-a-lifetime choice, and it is a decision that should be made carefully. Many communities allow prospective residents to experience life at the facility. Each community has an agreement or contract that lays out the services provided. You should make sure your client understands the contract before signing.

Tax Issues[1]   **10**

With all the options your clients have to choose from in planning their long-term care, there are, of course, tax implications. This chapter focuses on tax issues that appear routinely in an elder law practice, plan, or both.

The topics that we will discuss in this chapter include the following:

- Income taxation of social security
- The medical deduction
- Tax issues in gifting assets
- Powers of attorney
- Grantor trusts
- Tax implications of homeownership
- Promissory notes, intrafamily loans, and below market gift loan rules
- Nanny tax

Income Taxation of Social Security

Most elderly clients receive Social Security retirement benefits. Whether or not social security is subject to income taxes will depend on the balance of the clients' tax return; for example, a large distribution from a client's IRA may cause the social security to become taxable. There are two components to the mechanical rules relating to Social Security (SS). First, is the social security includable? And second, how much is includable?

To determine if your client's social security is included in their gross income, the following steps must be taken (see Internal Revenue Code (IRC) §86):

---

[1] Contributing author: David R. Okrent of 33 Walt Whitman Road, Suite 137, Dix Hills, NY 11746; Telephone:1-631-427-4600; E-mail: dokrent@ davidrokrentlaw.com.

1. Calculate *modified adjusted gross income* (MAGI). MAGI is your client's adjusted gross income without includible SS, excludible higher education savings bond interest, excludible adoption assistance payments, the IRC §199 domestic production activities, the IRC §221 deduction for interest on a qualified education loan, the IRC §222 deduction for higher education expenses, the IRC §911 exclusion from gross income for U.S. citizens or residents living abroad, excludible foreign earned income or housing amount, excludible income from U.S. possessions, the IRC §931 exclusion for income from American Samoa, excludible income from Puerto Rican sources available to bona fide residents of Puerto Rico, and an increased by any tax-exempt interest received or accrued by the taxpayer during the year.

2. Use your client's MAGI and add one-half of her social security to it. This is her *readjusted modified adjusted gross income* (RMAGI).

3. Compare your client's RMAGI to the appropriate base amount below in the following list; if RMAGI exceeds the base amount, she is a taxable individual (TI). The base amounts are
   - $32,000 for a joint return;
   - zero for married taxpayers who live together and file separately; and
   - $25,000 for all others. Unless a treaty exemption applies, non-resident aliens are TIs. See IRC §871(a)(3)(B).

If your client meets the first part and is a TI, then to determine how much social security is included in gross income (GI), take the following steps:

1. Compare your client's RMAGI to an *adjusted base* (AB) amount. The AB amounts are
   - $44,000 for a joint return;
   - zero for married taxpayers who live together and file separately; and
   - $34,000 for all others.

2. Then, use one of the following calculations:
   - If your client's RMAGI exceeds the AB, the amount of SS in GI is the lesser of one half of the SS or half of the RMAGI over the base amount.

Example A: Joan is unmarried. She received taxable interest of $14,000, tax-exempt interest of $15,000, and SS of $9,000. Joan's MAGI is $29,000 (including the taxable and tax-exempt interest but disregarding SS). Joan's RMAGI is $33,500 ($29,000 + 1/2 of $9,000). Joan's base amount is $25,000 and her AB is $34,000. She is a TI subject to the first alternative computation. The portion of SS in Joan's GI is $4,250, the lesser of $4,500 (1/2 of $9,000) or $4,250 (1/2 of the excess of $33,500 over $25,000).

- If your client's RMAGI does not exceeds the AB the amount of SS in GI is the lesser of 85 percent of the SS or the sum of 85 percent of the excess of the taxpayer's RMAGI over the AB plus the lesser of the amount determined under a. above or half of the difference between the taxpayer's base amount and AB. **Observation:** A TI subject to the second computation must also determine the amount under the first computation because it is a component of the second computation.

Example B: Joan has $20,000 of taxable interest, tax-exempt interest of $15,000, and SS of $10,000. Her MAGI is $35,000 (including the taxable and tax-exempt interest but disregarding SS). Her RMAGI is $40,000 ($35,000 + 1/2 of $10,000). Joan's base amount is $25,000 and her AB amount is $34,000. She is a TI subject to the second computation. Under the first computation, the portion of SS that would be included in her GI is $5,000, the lesser of $5,000 (1/2 of $10,000) or $7,500 (1/2 of the excess of $40,000 over $25,000). Half of the $9,000 difference between Joan's $25,000 base amount and the $34,000 AB amount is $4,500. The portion of SS included in her GI is $8,500, the lesser of $8,500 (85 percent of $10,000) or $9,600 ($5,100 [85 percent of the $6,000 excess of her $40,000 RMAGI over the $34,000 AB) plus $4,500 (the lesser of the $5,000 amount determined under a. above or the $4,500 difference between the base amount and AB amount]).

The Medical Deduction

A major focus of an elder law plan is the payment of medical care. It is important to know not only the fundamentals regarding medical expenses are deductible, but also the uniqueness of the deduction as it relates to such things as long-term care insurance, having a another person (such as a child) pay those expenses, or both.

Medical Deduction Overview

The medical deduction is provided in IRC §213. Under that section, individuals can deduct, as an itemized deduction, un-reimbursed medical expenses that exceed 7.5 percent of adjusted gross income. It includes amounts paid for diagnosis, cure, mitigation, treatment or prevention of disease, and for the purpose of affecting any structure or function of the body. Amounts for medicine and drugs are also included if individuals are prescribed drugs or insulin. Amounts paid for qualified long-term care services (as defined in IRC §7702B(c)),213(d)(1) for insurance (including Medicare part B premiums) covering said medical care, or for any qualified long-term care insurance contract (as defined in section 7702B(b)(10) [see below]) shall be taken into account.

Can legal fees qualify as a Medical deduction? In Carl A. Gerstacker v. Commissioner, 49 T.C. 522 (1968), rev'd 414 F.2d 448(1969), the United States Court of Appeals for the Sixth Circuit permitted a deduction for legal fees incurred in a guardianship proceeding. The court reasoned the legal fees incurred for his involuntary institutionalization through guardianship were attributable to his medical care and, therefore, were deductible, but the fees for handling the Guardianship estate were not (see Rev. Rul. 71-281, 1971-2 C.B. 165).

Expenses of Another

In many elder law plans, individuals other than the recipient of the medical care are, in some cases, the children of the elder patient who pay the medical bills for their parent. Individuals who pay for the care of another may be entitled to deduct the cost of such care on their tax return if they meet four requirements (IRC §152(a), Treas. Reg. §1.213-1(e)(3)):

1. First, they must pay more than one-half of the recipient's support for the calendar year. *Support* is determined yearly and includes the following:
    - The fair rental value of lodging
    - The cost of clothing, education, medical and dental care, gifts, transportation, church contributions, and entertainment and recreation expenses
    - A proportionate share of the expenses incurred in maintaining the family as a whole that can be directly attributable to each individual, such as food, but is not attributable to the overhead of the home, which may include electricity, repairs, and taxes (see Treas. Reg. §1.151-1).
2. Second, the recipient must have a special relationship to the payer (that is, is a parent or child).
3. Third, the recipient must have filed separately from her spouse.
4. Finally, the dependent must be a citizen, national, or resident of the United States or must be a resident of Canada or Mexico at some time during the calendar year in which the tax year of the taxpayer begins, or is an alien child adopted by and living with a U.S. citizen or national as a member of her household for the entire tax year.

Long-term Care

The IRC specifically defines what type of long-term care qualifies for a tax deduction, including rules relating to long-term care insurance. The rules usually include nursing home care and can be broad enough to include other types of care and facilities as well, such as assisted living care ordered by a doctor.

IRC §7702B(b)(10) defines qualified long-term care services as: (1) necessary diagnostic, preventative, therapeutic, curing, treating, mitigating and rehabilitative services, and maintenance or personal care services and (2) required by a chronically ill individual and provided pursuant to a plan of care prescribed by a licensed health care practitioner. An individual is chronically ill if she has been certified by a licensed health care practitioner within the previous 12 months as unable, for at least 90 days, to perform at least two *activities of daily living* (ADLs)—eating, toileting, transferring, bathing, dressing, and continence—without substantial assistance from another individual, due to loss of functional capacity, and without requiring substantial supervision to be protected from threats to health and safety due to severe cognitive impairment.

Qualified long-term care insurance contracts issued after 1996 are treated as accident and health insurance contracts (see IRC §7702B(a)(1)). Amounts (other than policyholder dividends, as defined in IRC §808 or premium refunds) received from such contracts are treated as amounts received for personal injury or sickness or as reimbursement for expenses actually incurred for medical care and are excludable, subject to a per diem limit.

QLTCC Requirements

A *qualified long-term care insurance contract* (QLTCC) is a contract that only covers qualified long-term care services and the following:

- Provides insurance coverage only for qualified long-term care services;
- Does not pay or reimburse expenses to the extent that the expenses are reimbursable under Medicare (or would be reimbursable but for a deductible or coinsurance amount). This requirement does not apply to expenses that are reimbursable under Medicare only as a secondary payor or the contract makes per diem or other periodic payments without regard to expenses;
- Is guaranteed renewable;
- Does not provide for a cash surrender value or other money that can be paid, assigned, pledged as collateral for a loan, or borrowed; and
- Provides that all refunds of premiums (other than refunds on the death of the insured or on a complete surrender or cancellation of the contract, which cannot exceed the aggregate premiums paid under the contract) and policyholder dividends or similar amounts are to be applied as a reduction of future premiums or as an increase of future benefits.

See IRC §7702B. The long-term care insurance contract must also take into account at least five out of six activities of daily living. For example, a contract can require that an individual be unable to perform two out of any five of the activities. But this requirement is not satisfied by a contract that requires that an individual be unable to perform two out of any four of the activities. This requirement concerning consideration of activities of daily living does not apply to the determination of whether an individual is a chronically ill individual either by virtue of severe cognitive impairment or if the insured satisfies a standard (if any) that is not based upon activities of daily living, as determined under Treasury Regulations (see Notice 97-31, 1997-1 CB 417). For a safe harbor rule on the continuation of pre-1997 long-term care insurance contract standards, see Treas. Reg. §1.7702B-2 and Notice 97-31, 1997-21 IRB 5.

A contract won't fail to qualify as a long-term care insurance contract because payments are made on a per diem or other periodic basis without regard to the expenses actually incurred in the period to which the payment relates. In addition, no provision of law is to be construed or applied so as to prohibit the offering of a qualified long-term care insurance contract on the basis that the contract coordinates its benefits with those provided under Medicare. The per diem limit for any period is the excess (if any) of the greater of $270 per day for 2008, the equivalent amount when payments are made on another periodic basis, or the costs incurred for qualified long-term care services provided for the insured for the period over the total payments received as reimbursement (by insurance or otherwise) for qualified long-term care services provided for the insured during the period (see IRC §7702B(d)(2)). If payments exceed this limit, the excess is excludible in income only to the extent of actual costs incurred for long-term care services; amounts with respect to which no such actual costs are incurred are fully includible.

If the taxpayer itemizes her deductions, the premiums qualify for the medical deduction, limited in 2008 to the following schedule illustrated in Table 10.1:

Table 10.1: Medical Deductions for 2008

Age	Deduction
Age 40 or under	$ 310
Age 41 to 50	$ 580
Age 51 to 60	$1,150
Age 61 to 70	$3,080
Age 71 or over	$3,850

Rev Proc 2007-66, Sec. 3.21, 2007-45 IRB .

Tax Issues in Gifting Assets

Frequently, elder law plans recommend the transfer of assets. Many times the manner in which assets are transferred (that is, outright or to a trust, etc.) is based on tax issues—not issues relating to governmental entitlements.

Gift and Estate Tax

Currently individuals can gift, up to a total of $1,000,000 during their lifetime for Federal Gift Tax purposes, without gift tax liability (see IRC § 2505). In addition, a donor can give the annual exclusion amount—currently $12,000 per donee per year—without affecting the $1,000,000 lifetime gift tax exemption (see IRC § 2503(b), Rev. Proc. 2006-53, 2006-48 I.R.B. 996, §3.32(1)). With respect to the Federal Estate tax, your client gets a gift tax exemption add-on, giving her a combined applicable exclusion amount of $2,000,000 for the years of 2006-2008 and of $3,500,000 for 2009. In 2010, the estate tax is eliminated, but there is a snap back in 2011 to $1,000,000, the 2001 applicable exclusion amount.

The elder law plan should account for the current exemption, but it is important to keep an eye towards the future. For example, in planning with spouses, the use of disclaimers under IRC §2518 to fund a credit shelter trust may be more appropriate than formulas. Formula funding typically will require an amount to be placed into the credit shelter trust upon the death of the first spouse. The amount is generally the applicable exclusion amount. The higher the exclusion amount becomes, the more likely it is that the trust will be funded. But there may be less need for the trust because the surviving spouse can have more upon her death. The disclaimer method permits the surviving spouse to determine the amount of assets, if any, to fund the credit shelter. This is done within nine months of death (see IRC § 2518).

In certain parts of the country, family homes have appreciated significantly in value, far beyond what the owners ever expected. In many cases, the home represents the major asset of the family. If lifetime gifts exceed $1,000,000 (with the exclusive of any annual exclusion gifts), a gift tax will be imposed. For example, if gifts total $1,100,000, the Federal Gift tax payable is $41,000.00. If no gifts were made and the asset is inherited in 2007 or 2008, there would be no tax, plus, as discussed in the following section "Income Tax Issues of Gifting Assets," there is a basis adjustment. In this scenario, if gifting is required, we would want to be able to give away the home for Medicaid purposes, but not for tax purposes. The most common way to protect the home for Medicaid planning purposes is through the use of an irrevocable trust in which the grantor has retained special or limited lifetime and testamentary powers of appointment. Such powers of appointment permit the grantor to retain the right to change the remainder beneficiaries to among a limited class, typically excluding the grantor, her spouse, and any other person or entity that would cause the trust to be considered available assets for government entitlement benefits such as Medicaid. This special power causes any transfer to the trust to be considered an *incomplete gift* for federal estate and gift tax purposes, but complete for all other purposes including government benefits (refer to Treas. Regs. §25.2511-2). Since the transfer of assets are incomplete lifetime gifts, they instead will be part the grantor's taxable estate upon her death. The inclusion in the grantor's taxable estate gives us a potential for a favorable basis adjustment (that is, a basis step-up) as discussed in the following section.

Income Tax Issues of Gifting Assets

When an elder law plan contemplates gifting assets, two questions must be resolved:

1. Is the built-in potential income tax on the appreciation of the asset greater than the estate tax that would be attributable to the asset if it were included in the estate?

2.   What should be done with items that are *income in respect of a decedent* (IRD)?

Built-In Potential Income Tax

The reason we need to address the built-in potential income tax on the appreciation of the asset is because of the conflicting competition among rules of basis regarding gifts and inheritances. The donee of a gift of a capital asset acquires the donor's basis if the fair market value is higher than donor's basis. If the fair market value is lower then donor's basis, for purposes of calculating a loss on sale of the asset by the donee, the basis is the lower fair market value. In comparison, the basis of an asset inherited by a beneficiary is the fair market value on date of death or alternate valuation date (see IRC §§1014, 1015). It is important to note that this rule changes in 2010, only to revert back in 2011 (refer to the prior section on "Gift and Estate Tax"). Assume that an individual has assets totaling $1,100,000—all of which are appreciated capital assets with a basis of zero. Upon the individual's death, there will be no federal estate tax, and, if the assets are sold at the estate tax value (the fair market value on date of death or alternate valuation date), there will be no income tax. If we assume that the individual made a gift of the entire $1,100,000 (ignoring the annual exclusions), a gift tax of $41,000 would be due, and, upon sale of the asset assuming a zero basis, the capital gains tax under current law would be approximately $165,000.00, resulting in a combined tax of $206,000. Obviously, from purely a tax perspective, gifting the asset outright appears to be a bad idea. An elder law plan must consider this and weigh it against the cost of long-term care. Again, that is precisely why highly appreciated homes and securities are often transferred to irrevocable trusts that contain special powers of appointment. If the real estate, securities, or both are not sold until death, the individual's heirs would receive a basis step-up at the time of death (see the prior section on "Gift and Estate Tax" regarding potential changes to the basis step-up rules in 2010).

Further complicating this is the potential for the loss of a tax benefit to which only the donor may be entitled—the personal residence capital gain exclusion under IRC §121. If the asset gifted is the donor's home, the personal residence capital gain exclusion is jeopardized. If the

donor is looking to protect her home for her lifetime, and is not motivated for estate and gift tax reasons to gift it away, the use of an irrevocable trust that also qualifies as a Grantor Trust as to corpus may be used
(see IRC §671 -679 and the following discussion on Grantor Trusts). By
using a Grantor Trust, the grantor will be deemed the owner and thereby
preserves the capital gain exclusion. Again, the use of the special power
of appointment causes the trust to meet this. Some practitioners prefer to
use Life Estates in real property rather than a Grantor Trust. However,
the use of life estate has significant drawbacks:

1. Transfer of the home to the transferree's children is deemed a full
   value gift for Federal Gift Tax Purposes (see IRC §2702).
2. If the property is sold during the life tenant's lifetime, there may be
   a capital gains tax, and part or all of the capital gain exclusion for
   a personal residence may be lost (see IRC §121).
3. The sale of a home in which a senior holds a life estate can cause the
   value of the life estate to be deemed an available asset for Medicaid
   purposes and could disqualify an individual from benefits.

Income in Respect of a Decedent (IRD)

Many clients have significant assets tied up in retirement vehicles, such
as IRAs. If a beneficiary inherits these vehicles, under IRC §691(a) they
are labeled IRDs and are taxable income to the beneficiary when the
IRA, etc., is actually required to be distributed. IRD includes items that
are

- includible in a decedent's estate for federal estate tax purposes and
- includible as gross income for the beneficiaries when realized.

Many seniors are faced with the dilemma of how to handle these
assets. In creating an appropriate plan, the primary question is whether
they should distribute the asset during their lifetimes, pay the related
income taxes, and gift or leave the balance to their heirs. This seems to
make tax sense if the senior is in a lower income tax bracket. However,
to maintain her quality of life, the senior may need this money working
for her on a tax-deferred basis.

The following is a brief list of things to consider when it comes to IRD plans:

1.   What is the tax bracket of the senior versus her heirs?
2.   Does the senior have tax deductions (that is, medical expenses) to offset the income?
3.   Will the distribution cause other income to become taxable, for example, make social security taxable?
4.   Does the senior need the money to grow in a tax-deferred status to maintain her quality of life?
5.   How does the state's Medicaid program treat retirement plan assets? For example, does Medicaid ignore the principal balance of the retirement account and only count as income the minimum required distribution?
6.   Is the estate a taxable estate in that the beneficiary may be able to get some relief by claiming an itemized deduction for any estate tax attributable to IRD (IRC §691(c))? Note that due to the difference in tax rates for estate tax and income tax, however, it is generally not balanced.

Powers of Attorney

A *power of attorney* (POA) is a document that an individual uses to designate another individual or entity to make financial decisions for her. A POA creates a principal-agency relationship. The individual or entity appointed is called the *agent*, and the individual making the appointment is the *principal*. A *durable power of attorney* (DPOA) is one that stays in affect when the principal becomes incapacitated.

Relation to Tax Matters

With respect to tax items, a principal may authorize an agent under a DPOA to

- inspect any tax return or information return (see IRC §6103(e)(6));
- sign income tax returns if the principal is unable to sign by reason of disease, injury, or continuous absence from the United States for a period of at least 60 days prior to the due date of the return (see IRC §6012(b)(2)); or

- negotiate checks payable for tax refunds (see 31 C.F.R. §240.15(b)(2)).

However, only certain agents, known as *recognized representatives*, may represent the principal before the IRS. A recognized representative is an individual who is appointed under a POA or DPOA and is one of the following:

- An attorney
- A certified public accountant
- An enrolled agent
- An enrolled actuary
- Certain other individuals who may include immediate family members

For tax matters, a POA, a DPOA, or both must contain the following information:

- Name and address of the taxpayer
- Identification number of the taxpayer
- Name and address of the recognized representative
- Description of the matter(s) for which representation is authorized

The description of the matter(s) must include the following:

- The type of tax involved
- The federal tax form number
- The specific year(s)/period(s) involved
- A clear expression of the taxpayer's intention concerning the scope of authority granted to the recognized representative

See Treas. Regs. §601.503(a) for more details.

The IRS will accept the following POA or DPA documents for tax matters (see Regs. §601.503(b):

- A properly completed and executed IRS Form 2848.
- A POA or DPOA, other than IRS Form 2848, provided that it contains the information described in the previous list. However, a completed IRS Form 2848, signed by the recognized representative, must be attached for purposes of processing. The taxpayer need not sign IRS Form 2848.

If the POA or DPOA fails to include all of the information required, then the recognized representative can cure this defect by executing IRS Form 2848 (on behalf of the taxpayer) that includes the missing information. Attaching a copy of the POA or DPA to the IRS Form 2848 will validate the POA or DPA, provided that the following conditions are satisfied:

- The POA or DPA contemplates authorization to handle, among other things, federal tax matters.
- The agent attaches a statement (signed under a penalty of perjury) to IRS Form 2848 that states that the POA or DPA is valid under state law.

Tax Ramifications of a POA or DPOA

A POA or DPOA used in an elder law plan context usually contains very broad powers, such as a power permitting the agent to gift assets to herself. The agent under this document is said to have a *power to appoint* because she can appoint the principal assets to herself. Is the granting of this power a gift in and of itself, if the agent gifts the principal's assets to a person other than herself? Would the agent be viewed as making a gift since she gave up the right to appoint the asset to herself? This section will review these issues.

The granting of a POA or DPOA with an unlimited gifting power is not a taxable gift by the principal as long as it is revocable (refer to Treas. Regs. §25.2511-2(c)). In addition, a POA or DPOA must rise to the point of being considered a *general power of appointment* for there to be tax issues. A general power of appointment is one in which the person holding the power (that is, the agent) can exercise it in favor of herself, her estate, her creditors, or the creditors of her estate and property subject to its inclusion in the estate of a deceased power holder or, if the power is exercised during the lifetime of the power holder, its inclusion as a gift by the power holder (see Treas. Regs. §§2041, 2514). If this is an unintended tax consequence, it is prudent for many reasons to make sure the POA or DPOA is limited so that the power does not rise to the level of a *general power of appointment*.

POA and DPOA Considerations

The POA or DPOA can

1. prohibit gifts to the agent herself;.
2. limit gifts to the greater of $5,000.00 or 5 percent of the assets covered by the power (This is a *deminimis limitation* found in the IRC [see IRC §2514].);
3. limit gifts to the annual exclusion amount under IRC §2503(b);
4. limit gifts to the agent by an ascertainable standard related to health, education, maintenance, or support;
5. authorize a disinterested third party to make gifts to the principal's family;
6. require the agent to obtain the consent or joinder of the principal (although this would defeat the purpose of a DPOA if the principal becomes incompetent); and
7. require the agent to obtain the consent or joinder of a person with a substantial interest (that is, a residuary beneficiary under the principal's will).

The author prefers the last option since it will serve all planning needs as it doesn't limit the gifting provided that the children (who are the usual agents) are getting along.

Grantor Trusts

The income taxation of a trust is very complex. Perhaps the most complex part is determining who the taxpayer is. Under the IRC, the taxpayer can be the trust, the grantor, or a third party with certain rights in the trust. In the elder law plan, one typically wants trust income to be taxed to the grantor, which intentionally violates one of the Grantor Trust rules in IRC §§671-679. A grantor trust is any trust that contains certain prohibited powers, under IRC §§671-679, and that trust income is taxed as if the trust were owned in whole or in part by the grantor of the trust. The grantor is required to include in her personal income tax computations those items of income, deduction, and credit allocable to any portion of a trust that a grantor or third person is deemed to own. In an elder law plan this is typically a good thing, especially if the estate is under the applicable exemption amount. It eliminates the need for trust return filings—other than the first year—and preserves the client's tax attributes relating to the property, such as the $250,000 capital gain exclusion of the sale of the primary residence.

The most common method of creating a grantor trust is through the use of a *special power of appointment* over the remainder of the trust. As previously discussed, this power makes any transfer to the trust incomplete for gift tax purposes. This power also causes the trust to be a grantor trust (see IRC §674).

Tax Implications of Home Ownership

IRC §121 (as amended by the Taxpayer Relief Act of 1997) provides the most important rule in this area: Taxpayers may exclude from income up to $250,000 ($500,000 for taxpayers filing joint returns) of gain from the sale of a residence. The residence must have been owned and used by the taxpayer as her principal residence for periods aggregating two years during the five-year period preceding the sale. The exclusion is allowed each time a taxpayer meets the eligibility requirements, but generally no more frequently than once every two years. The age requirement under the pre-1997 Act is eliminated. This section also replaces the rollover rule of former IRC §1034, generally effective for sales occurring after May 6, 1997.

Former IRC §1034 (as it read prior to repeal in 1997) provided rules for the non-recognition of gain when a taxpayer sold a residence and, within two years either before or after the sale, replaced it with a new residence with an adjusted sales price greater than that of the old residence. Both the old and new residences had to be used by the taxpayer as her principal residence if former IRC §1034 was to apply. Former IRC §1034 is of only very limited relevance for taxable years beginning in 1998 and after. A special rule, applicable only to personal residences, should be noted for pre-May 1997 dispositions, acquisitions, or both of residences. If gain was not recognized on the sale or exchange of a principal residence under former IRC §1034 because the taxpayer purchased or constructed another principal residence within the statutory replacement period, the basis of the new residence was reduced by an amount equal to the realized gain not recognized—that is, the unrecognized gain was rolled over into the replacement property through a lower basis in that property (see former IRC §1034(e)).

IRC Section 163(h) provides another important provision in this area. It excepts from the disallowance of personal interest deductions any qualified residence interest paid or accrued by a taxpayer. Qualified residence interest includes *acquisition indebtedness* (that is, debt secured by the taxpayer's residence that is incurred to acquire, construct, or substantially improve that residence) and *home equity indebtedness* (which is debt secured by the residence that does not exceed the fair market value of the residence less any acquisition indebtedness limited to $100,000).

Exclusion of Gain on Sale of Residence: 1997 Taxpayer Relief Act IRC §121

A taxpayer's principal residence is a capital asset. Upon the sale of a principal residence, the taxpayer realizes capital gain or loss. However, no loss is recognized, because a residence is personal in nature. In the case of a sale that produces gain, IRC §121 of the Code (as amended by the Taxpayer Relief Act of 1997) provides an exclusion from income for a portion of such gain. Prior to the 1997 Act, two special tax provisions were used to defer or exclude the recognition of such gain: the former home sale rollover rule and the former over-55 exclusion rule. The latter two provisions have now been repealed.

Backing up a bit, the sale of real property is normally a taxable event; however, an exclusion from gross income under IRC §121 may be available in the case of a sale of the taxpayer's principal residence that qualifies for such treatment. The term *principal residence* is not defined in the statute. The regulations indicate that all the facts and circumstances must be examined in view of key circumstances that include a taxpayer's place of employment and principal place of residence. The home-sale gain exclusion rule generally allows a taxpayer to exclude gain from gross income realized from the sale or exchange of property if, during the five-year period ending on the date of the sale or exchange, such property has been owned and used by the taxpayer as the taxpayer's principal residence for a period aggregating two or more years. The amount of the exclusion from gross income is generally limited to $250,000 for individuals and $500,000 for certain married taxpayers filing a joint return. The exclusion is allowed each time a taxpayer meets the eligibility requirements, but generally no more frequently than once every two years.

Among the types of property that will qualify for the IRC §121 exclusion as a residence are a houseboat, house trailer, and the stock held by a tenant stockholder in a cooperative housing corporation (see former Treas. Regs. §1.1034-1(c)(3)(i); Lokan v. Comr., T.C. Memo 1979-380; H.R. Rep. No. 586, 82nd Cong., 1st Sess., 1951-2 C.B. 378, 436). Furniture and other personal property will not qualify for IRC §121 treatment.

The amount of gain that may be excluded from gross income generally cannot exceed $250,000 for individual taxpayers and $500,000 in the case of married couples if a joint return is filed for the taxable year of sale. Either spouse can meet the ownership requirement with respect to the sale of the residence, provided that both spouses meet the aggregate use requirement and neither spouse is ineligible for the benefits. In the event of the death of a spouse, the surviving spouse can file a joint return with the decedent only for the year of death, and therefore she take the full $500,000 exclusion (but the residence must be sold in the year of the decedent's death in order to do so).

The home-sale exclusion provision can generally be used no more than once every two years. In the case of joint filers not sharing a principal residence, an exclusion of $250,000 is available on a qualifying sale of the residence of one of the spouses. The rule limiting the exclusion to only one sale every two years by the taxpayer does not prevent a husband and wife from filing a joint return with each return excluding up to $250,000 of gain from the sale or exchange of each spouse's principal residence provided that each spouse would be permitted to exclude up to $250,000 of gain if they filed separate returns. If a single taxpayer who is otherwise eligible for an exclusion marries someone who has used the exclusion within the two-year period prior to the marriage, the taxpayer remains eligible for a maximum exclusion of $250,000. If a married couple filing a joint return does not qualify for the $500,000 maximum exclusion, the amount of the maximum exclusion that may be claimed by the couple is the sum of each spouse's maximum exclusion determined on a separate basis.

It is not necessary that the taxpayer use the property as a principal residence at the time of the sale. Instead, all that is required is that the ownership and use tests as a principal residence set forth in IRC §121 during the five-year testing period be satisfied. The periods of use as a principal residence and ownership need not be concurrent, that is, use as a principal residence by the taxpayer as a tenant qualifies, so long as the ownership requirement is independently satisfied. A taxpayer's period of use of a principal residence includes certain periods during which the taxpayer resides in a qualified facility any time during the five-year period before the sale or exchange of the residence (see IRC §121(d)(7). Regs. §1.121-1(c)). This provision applies where a taxpayer becomes physically or mentally incapable of self-care, owns property, and uses such property as a principal residence during a five-year period for periods aggregating at least one year during that period. A qualified facility is defined as any institution, including a nursing home, licensed by a state or political subdivision to care for incapacitated individuals.

An unmarried widower or widow-taxpayer's period of ownership and use of a principal residence includes the period for which the taxpayer's deceased spouse owned and used such residence for purposes of the home-sale exclusion provision (see IRC §121(d)(2). Regs. §1.121-4(a)(1)).

Where a principal residence was acquired in a transaction covered by the former IRC §1034 rollover provision, the aggregate periods of ownership and use of the taxpayer's prior residence (including each prior residence taken into account in determining the holding period of such residence) are taken into account in determining ownership and use of the current residence (see IRC §121(g). Regs. §1.121-4(h)).

Where a trust owns a residence and ownership of the trust (or the portion of the trust that includes the residence) is imputed for tax purposes to an individual (that is, a grantor trust), that individual is treated as the owner of the residence (see Treas. Regs. §1.121-1(c)(3) and PLR 199912026). This result also occurs under former IRC §121 (see Rev. Rul. 85-45, 1985-1 C.B. 183. As to former IRC §1034, see Rev. Rul. 66-159, 1966-1 C.B. 162). This permits the exclusion of any gain under IRC §121 when the residence is sold. By contrast, where a residence is owned by an irrevocable non-grantor trust, it is the IRS's position that the trust is ineligible to claim the benefits of IRC §121.

In PLR 200104005, the residence had been placed in a revocable trust by the husband and wife that owned the residence. Upon the death of one of the spouses, the revocable trust split into two parts—one of which became irrevocable. The residence was placed in this irrevocable part, with the surviving spouse receiving a lifetime right to occupy the residence. The trust eventually sold the residence and sought a ruling that IRC §121 shielded a portion of the gain. The IRS ruled otherwise, even though the surviving spouse had occupied the residence for over 30 years and had a power to direct sale. Instead, according to the IRS, the IRC §121 exclusion was only applicable to the portion the surviving spouse was deemed to own under a "five or five" withdrawal power contained in the trust.

A similar result was reached in PLR 200018021 where the taxpayer was an individual who was the income beneficiary of a trust holding the residence. The IRS ruled that IRC §121 was not applicable because the individual taxpayer did not own the residence. Thus, although at first blush the result in PLR 200018021 seems somewhat inconsistent with the language of IRC §121(d)(8), there is really no inconsistency. Section 121(d)(8) is directed at the situation where an individual taxpayer actually owns the remainder interest in the residence, while PLR 200018021 denies IRC §121 treatment where the actual owner of the residence is a trust with the taxpayer only having a life estate *in the trust.*

Section 121(d)(10) extends the benefits of IRC §121 to the sale of a principal residence by estates, heirs, and certain grantor trusts relative to decedents who die after 2009. Under IRC §121(d)(10), ownership and use by the decedent is deemed to be ownership and use by the respective successor; in the case of an individual successor, the ownership and use by the decedent can be tacked on to that of the individual successor.

Principal residence status under IRC §121 will be determined after review of all the facts and circumstances. The term *principal residence* should have the same meaning as it does under former IRC §1034. However, the statutory reference to principal residence must be read subject to the special requirements of IRC §121.

While the regulations do not resolve all issues in this regard, they do offer some guidance on the sale of vacant land. Treas. Regs. §1.121-1(b)(3)(i) provides that as long as a sale of the taxpayer's principal residence occurs within two years of the land sale, both will qualify for the IRC §121 exclusion. In effect, the two (or more) sales are treated as one. Gain relative to the dwelling unit is excluded first.

When a taxpayer can satisfy the two-year ownership and use requirements only for a portion of the property sold, only the gain attributable to that portion is excludible under IRC §121(a).

Sale of a Partial Interest

Sometimes a client may wish to sell only a partial interest in her principal residence (for example, a child selling a parent the right to live in the home for the remainder of the parent's life). This technique has become especially attractive after the Deficit Reduction Act of 2006 codified the sale of a life estate as a transfer for value if certain other requirements are met.

A taxpayer may apply §121's exclusion to a gain from the sale or exchange of an interest in the taxpayer's principal residence that is less than the taxpayer's entire interest if the interest sold or exchanged includes an interest in the residence (see IRC §121(d)(8)(A). Regs. §1.121-4(e) and Rev. Rul. 84-43, 1984-1 C.B. 27).

For purposes of section 121(b)(1) and (2) (relating to the maximum limitation amount of the section 121 exclusion), sales or exchanges of partial interests in the same principal residence are treated as one sale or exchange. Therefore, only one maximum limitation amount of $250,000 ($500,000 for certain joint returns) applies to the combined sales or exchanges of the partial interests. In applying the maximum limitation amount to sales or exchanges that occur in different taxable years, a taxpayer may exclude gain from the first sale or exchange of a partial interest up to the taxpayer's full maximum limitation amount and may exclude gain from the sale or exchange of any other partial interest in the same principal residence to the extent of any remaining maximum limitation amount. Each spouse is treated as excluding one-half of the gain from a sale or exchange to which section 121(b)(2)(A) and section 1.121-2(a)(3)(i) (relating to the limitation for certain joint returns) apply.

For purposes of applying section 121(b)(3) (restricting the application of section 121 to only 1 sale or exchange every 2 years), each sale or exchange of a partial interest is disregarded with respect to other sales or exchanges of partial interests in the same principal residence, but is taken into account as of the date of the sale or exchange in applying section 121(b)(3) to that sale or exchange and the sale or exchange of any other principal residence (see Reg's. §1.121-4(e)(3)). For example, in 1991, Taxpayer A buys a house that A uses as her principal residence. In 2004,

A's friend B moves into A's house and A sells B a 50 percent interest in the house, thus, realizing a gain of $136,000. A may exclude the $136,000 of gain. In 2005, A sells her remaining 50 percent interest in the home to B realizing a gain of $138,000. A may exclude $114,000 ($250,000 – $136,000 gain previously excluded) of the $138,000 gain from the sale of the remaining interest.

A taxpayer may elect, except to a person that bears a relationship to the taxpayer that is described in section 267(b) or 707(b), to apply the section 121 exclusion to gain from the sale or exchange of a remainder interest in the taxpayer's principal residence. If a taxpayer elects to exclude gain from the sale or exchange of a remainder interest in the taxpayer's principal residence, the section 121 exclusion will not apply to a sale or exchange of any other interest in the residence that is sold or exchanged separately. A taxpayer may make or revoke the election at any time before the expiration of a three-year period beginning on the last date prescribed by law (determined without regard to extensions) for the filing of the return for the taxable year in which the sale or exchange occurred. For example, if a taxpayer sells remainder interest to a friend and elects to use her exclusion, if the next year the taxpayer sells life estate to a different friend, the taxpayer cannot use the balance.

This is not inconsistent with the result in PLR 200018021 where the IRS denied IRC §121 treatment to the holder of a life estate in a trust that owned a residence. In PLR 200018021, the trust (and not the taxpayer) owned the property, and the IRS had long held former IRC §1034 and former IRC §121 inapplicable to trusts (other than grantor trusts). By contrast, the IRC §121(d)(8) election applies to situations where the principal residence is owned by one or more individuals.

The IRC §121(d)(8) election does not eliminate any of the other requirements of the IRC §121, such as the use of a principal residence requirement. Thus, the two situations where the IRC §121(d)(8) election seems most useful would be where either (a) the life tenant and the remainderman both simultaneously use the residence as their principal residence, or (b) an existing owner who already satisfies the use requirement sells a remainder interest to a third party.

Whether the IRS will permit a remainderman who simultaneously occupy the residence along with the life tenant to thereby satisfy the use requirement is unclear. In PLR 8246123, the IRS denied former IRC §1034 treatment to such a remainderman, concluding that the statutory requirement of use presumes a legal right to occupy—as opposed to a non-legal permissive occupation of the residence. IRC §121, of course, has its own use requirement that appears to parallel that of former IRC §1034.

The other situation is where a single individual owner who satisfies the use requirements bifurcates an existing ownership into a life estate and a remainder. In such circumstances, the sale of either the life estate or the sale of the remainder (assuming the IRC §121(d)(8) election) should qualify. The IRC §121(d)(8) election would presumably permit more gain to be sheltered if the remainder interest has substantially more value than the life interest because of the relative shortness of the life expectancy of the life by which the duration of the estate is measured. Note that the making of a IRC §121(d)(8) election to apply IRC §121 to the sale of the remainder interest precludes application of IRC §121 to any other interest in the residence (for example, the life estate).

As noted above, if one is not in the context of a IRC §121(d)(8) election, only the sale of the life estate can presumably qualify under IRC §121. In all likelihood, the residence will be sold on a unitary basis (that is, both remainderman and life tenant join in the sale) rather than the life estate being sold on a stand-alone basis. Assuming a unitary sale does occur, a portion of any sale gain would presumably have to be allocable to the remainder interest and a portion to the life estate. The result (again absent IRC §121(d)(8) election), therefore, is that only a portion of any gain can be excluded under IRC §121 (by the life tenant). The allocation between the two estates would presumably occur under the IRS actuarial tables. What this means in practicality is that a portion of the gain cannot be sheltered under IRC §121. So, if the taxpayer sells a life estate to a mother and remainder to the mother's child, absent the election only, the life estate portion would be covered by the exclusion.

Comment: If ownership of the life estate and remainder interests are unified and held by a single individual prior to the sale, it is unclear how the use test would be applied. An example would be where the owner of the life estate gives that estate to the remainderman. An argument exists that if the holding period of the life estate tacks on to that of the remainderman, then the period of use by the life tenant should tack on to that of the remainderman as well. The problem with this argument is that nothing within IRC §121 links the use requirement of IRC §121 with the concept of a holding period for capital gains purpose. The more likely result is that, in this example, the remainderman would have to begin her use period on the day that she first began occupying the residence as a principal residence after the gift of the life estate. A closer case is presented if it is the remainderman who gifts the remainder to the life tenant. In such circumstances the life tenant would likely already have satisfied the use requirement (albeit in the capacity as life tenant). It is simply unclear whether the portion of gain attributable to the former remainder interest can be excluded under IRC §121, because the life tenant did not own (and hence could not use this interest in the residence previously).

Sale of Remainder and/or Life Estates

Because of changes in Medicaid in 2006 as a result of the enactment of the Deficity Reduction Act of 2005, the sale of a life estate in a child's residence to a parent or sale of reminder interest in the parent's residence have become more popular. Some tangential and esoteric tax issues that revolve around that sale of an interest in property include the following questions:

- How does IRC §2702 apply?
- What are the related parties' basis in their reflective interests in the property?
- Is there a taxable event upon the natural termination of the interest?

Example C

Father (F) sells a remainder interest in an apartment building to Daughter (D). F is age 70. The value of the property is $1 million. The pertinent actuarial tables indicate that the remainder interest in such property should be sold for a specified percentage of its fair market value. Before the enactment of §2702, the remainder could be valued using the applicable actuarial tables and the §7520 interest rate (see §7520). Regs. §20.7520-1(a)(1) refers to the valuation tables for remainder in Regs. §20.2031-7(d) (see Regs. §20.2031-7(d)(7) providing Table S (single life remainder factors) applicable after April 30, 1999). After the enactment of §2702, where the transfer takes between family members, this valuation approach may not be available.

One object of these techniques is to eliminate the asset from the seller's gross estate. This result is sought because at the time of death

- the life tenant's life estate terminates, leaving no continuing value to be transferred, and
- the seller is not treated as the owner of the remainder interest in the transferred property.

As noted below, however, these objectives are quite difficult to accomplish under current federal tax rules. Let us evaluate these a little closer.

Estate and Gift Tax Considerations

Where a sale to a family member is involved and the transferor has retained an interest, IRC §2702 will need to be considered. This remainder interest sale transaction will often result in a taxable gift because of IRC §2702 gift tax valuation rules. Under IRC §2702 the seller is treated as transferring the entire property in exchange for the consideration paid by the remainder beneficiary unless the retained interest is a *qualified interest*. Family members include an individual's spouse, any ancestor or lineal descendant of the individual or the individual's spouse, any brother or sister of the individual, and any spouse of any individual described in subparagraph (B) or (C); attribution rules also apply. A qualified interest means any interest that consists of the right to receive fixed amounts payable not less frequently than annually, any interest that consists of the right to receive amounts that are payable not less frequently than annually and are a fixed percentage of the fair market value of the property in the trust (determined annually), and any non-contingent remainder interest if all of the other interests in the trust consist of interests described in paragraph (1) or (2). In addition, IRC §2702(c) states that where there is a transfer of an interest in property with respect to whether there is one or more term interests, the transfers will be treated as transfers of interest in a trust and will be define a term interest as a life interest in property or as an interest in property for a term of years.

Certain transfers escape §2702 and are valued using ordinary gift tax principles. Section 2702 does not apply if (1) the entire transfer is *incomplete* for gift tax purposes because of a retained power; or (2) the property is used as a personal residence by persons holding life or term interests in the property. The regulations state for a transfer to qualify under exception (2) it must be in conjunction with each of the following two trusts: a personal residence trust or a qualified personal residence trust. A life estate in the property itself does not appear to fit into either of these definitions and therefore would not qualify under the Treasury Departments interpretation (see Reg. §25.2702-5).

If §2702 applies, and the retained corpus interest is not a qualified interest, the value of the retained reversion will be deemed to be zero for gift tax purposes, thereby increasing pro tanto the amount of the gift, or, if the life estate is transferred for consideration, it makes the transaction a part-sale part-gift transaction.

Upon a sale of a remainder interest, the seller retains the life interest in the property. This life interest ordinarily is retained by the seller until the time of the seller's death. If the asset is transferred for full and adequate consideration, no estate tax inclusion ordinarily is required. Section 2036(a) provides that an asset conveyed during life is included in the transferor's gross estate if the transferor retained a life interest in the property transferred. Section 2036(a) further provides for its inapplicability where the property transfer was for full and adequate consideration.

The initial estate tax result is that, if the transfer is for consideration that is less than adequate and full consideration in money or money's worth, the transferred asset is included in the transferor's gross estate at its then fair market value (or as of the alternate valuation date) less the actual amount of consideration received. Gradow v. U.S., 897 F.2d 516 (Fed. Cir. 1990), aff'g 11 Cl. Ct. 808 (1987), held that, in a sale of a remainder interest, the existence of full and adequate consideration must be measured against the total value of the property, not just against the value of the remainder interest sold. Thus, under the Gradow theory, the sale of a remainder interest in property does not remove the property from the owner's estate unless the owner receives consideration equal to the total value of the property. The IRS was initially successful in using the Gradow argument in D'Ambrosio Est. v. Comr., 105 T.C. 252 (1995), rev'd and rem'd, 101 F.3d 309 (3d Cir. 1996), cert. denied, 520 U.S. 1230 (1997), where the Tax Court held that the entire value of closely held stock was includible in the decedent's estate, even though the decedent sold her remainder interest for an amount equal to its actuarial value, because the decedent had not received consideration in an amount equal to the full value of the stock. In determining the value of the property includible in the decedent's estate, the court subtracted the value of the consideration agreed on for the remainder purchase. The Third Circuit, rejecting the Gradow rationale, reversed and held that the adequacy of the consideration is evaluated on the date of the transfer by comparing the value of the remainder transferred to the value of the consideration received. The Third Circuit was joined in its conclusion in D'Ambrosio by the Fifth and Ninth Circuits. In Wheeler v. U.S., 116 F.3d 749 (5th Cir. 1997), the Fifth Circuit concluded that the decedent's sale to his sons of the remainder interest in his ranch was a bona fide sale for full and adequate consideration that took the property out of his estate. In Magnin Est. v. Comr. 184 F.3d 1074 (9th Cir. 1999), the court also held that "adequate and full consideration" is measured against the actuarial value of the remainder interest, rather than the fee-simple value of the property transferred, and remanded the case to the Tax Court for a finding on the value, at the time of the transaction, of the remainder interest and the consideration received in exchange for it. For a decedent outside these circuits, the IRS will probably seek to include in the seller's gross estate the full value of the property less the fair market value of the consideration for the sale of the remainder interest provided by a younger generation member.

Note: IRC §2702 is a gift tax provision and should not apply under IRC §2036 to alter the definition of adequate and full consideration in money or money's worth. Therefore, if an interest is transferred for an amount equal to its actuarial value, and IRC §2702 applies and treats the retained interest as zero (0) for gift tax purposes, the property should not later be included in the estate under IRC §2036 for failing the adequate and full consideration in money or money's worth solely based upon IRC §2702.

Income Tax Considerations

As already noted, the sale of the remainder interest or life estate will result in the realization of capital gain or loss to the seller. In determining the amount of gain or loss, the seller's basis for the property must be apportioned between the remainder interest sold and the retained life estate (or vice versa).

However, a special rule applies where part or all of a term interest (that is, a life estate) is received in a manner whereby the basis would be determined in accordance IRC §1014 (inherited basis), 1015 (gift basis), or 1041 (incident to divorce). In those instances, the basis attributable to such part received in said manner is treated as zero, unless the term interest together with all other interests in said property are conveyed at the same time. If all interests in the property are conveyed at the same time, then this rule does not apply and basis is determined normally (see Regs. §1.1014-5(a)(3). Cf., §1001(e)). For example, a woman leaves her husband a life estate in the home she owns by her last will. If she tries to sell this life estate alone, her basis is zero; however, if the entire house is sold, she will have an inherited basis.

Would the valuation rules under IRC §2702 impact the sale of a life estate? The answer should be no. First, the rule only applies to the value of the retained term interest. Second, IRC §2702 focuses on the value of the retained interest and not on the basis in said interest for income tax purposes.

Where the sale is between *related persons*, any loss is disallowed (see §267(a)(1) and §267(b) for determining those relationships that cause the applicability of this loss disallowance provision).

The IRS may argue that, upon the life tenant's death, the receipt of the property (unencumbered by a life estate) by the remainder beneficiary constitutes the realization of income to the remainder beneficiary (which should be recognized for income tax purposes). What has economically occurred in such a situation is that, upon the termination of the life interest, the remainder interest might be treated as being exchanged for the property itself.

If the property interest fully obtained upon termination of the life interest is not cash or a cash equivalent, the argument might be made that no income realization event occurred. If, however, the remainder interest is transformed into the equivalent of cash at the death of the life tenant, the IRS's position might be that a realization event requiring income recognition occurred at that time (see Guthrie v. Comr., 42 B.T.A. 696 (1940); Jones v. Comr., 40 T.C. 249 (1963), vac'd and rem'd, 330 F.2d 302 (3d Cir. 1964), on remand, T.C. Memo 1966-136). However, the better argument would seem to be that this is merely equivalent to perfecting title in property, not being a realization event for income tax purposes. These cases focused upon the sale of the remainder interest after the termination of the life estate, and they concluded that part of the proceeds would be considered ordinary income and part would be capital gain based upon an allocation between this second part, which is attributable to a discount in purchase price when the remainder interest was purchased due to the life estate.

Promissory Notes, Intrafamily Loans, and Below Market Gift Loan Rules

If an interest-free loan of money (or *below market* loan) is made in a family context, applicable federal tax rules require the re-characterization of these loans premised upon an arm's-length transaction to occur. Before the enactment of §7872, the Supreme Court in the Dickman v. Comr., 465 U.S. 330 (1984) held that an interest-free loan results in a gift from the lender to the borrower for federal gift tax purposes.

Gift Tax Issues

The IRS enunciated its gift timing and valuation position in litigating these gift and interest-free loan cases prior to IRC §7872. In the case of a *demand loan*, the amount of the gift was deemed to be the value of the right to the use of the money for a portion of the year as the lender allowed the borrower the interest-free use of the money (see Rev. Rul. 73-61, 1973-2 C.B. 408). Under this approach the amount of the gift was calculable as of the last day of each calendar year during which the loan was outstanding. In the context of a *term loan*, the amount of the gift transfer was the excess at the time of the loan of the amount of money borrowed over the then present value of the principal and interest payments to be made under the terms of the loan (see Rev. Rul. 81-286, 1981-2 C.B. 176; Dickman v. Comr., 465 U.S. 330 (1984)).

With the enactment of IRC §7872, the amount of the deemed payment from the lender to the borrower is to be determined solely under this Code provision. This provision is applicable to both income tax and gift tax determinations.

Below Market Loan Tax Principles

Conceptual Framework

Section 7872 relates to the tax treatment of loans that, in substance, result in a gift, payment of compensation, dividend, capital contribution or other similar payment from the lender to the borrower. Loans that are subject to this provision and do not require the payment of any interest or interest payments at a rate below the statutory rate (that is, below the applicable federal rate), are recharacterized as an arm's length transaction in which the lender made a loan to the borrower in exchange for a note requiring the payment of interest at the applicable federal rate.

Qualifications for Below Market Loans

Qualifications for below market loans include the following:

1. The borrower paid interest to the lender that (for income tax purposes)
   a. may be deductible to the borrower and
   b. is includible in income by the lender.
2. The lender (at the inception of this transaction)
   a. made a gift subject to the gift tax (in the case of a gratuitous transaction, as noted above);
   b. paid a dividend (in the case of a below market interest loan from the corporation to a shareholder);
   c. made a capital contribution (in the case of a below market interest loan to a corporation from a shareholder);
   d. paid compensation (in the case of a below market interest loan by an employer to a person providing services); or
   e. because of a below interest loan, made some other payment characterized in accordance with the true, economic substance of the transaction.

Gift Tax Rules

In the case of a demand loan, the lender is treated as transferring to the borrower and the borrower is treated as receiving from the lender, for gift tax purposes, an amount equal to the foregone interest on an annual basis as of the last day of the calendar year. With a gift loan (that is, a term loan) for gift tax purposes, the lender is treated as transferring to the borrower and the borrower is treated as receiving from the lender an amount equal to the excess of the amount of the loan over the present value of all principal and interest payments due under the loan. That gift amount is treated as transferred as of the date that the loan is made.

Income Tax Rules

For income tax purposes, with a demand loan, the donee, borrower, or both are treated as transferring to the lender, and the lender is treated as receiving from the borrower an amount equal to the foregone interest.

These events are treated as occurring on an annual basis as of the last day of the calendar year. Consequently, this foregone interest is included in income by the lender and is deductible by the borrower to the same extent as interest actually due on the loan from the borrower.

As noted above, the adequacy of any stated interest and the amount of any deemed payments are determined by reference to an applicable federal rate (see IRC §7872(e), prescribing applicability of the *applicable federal rate*). As specified in IRC §7872(f)(2), this rate is determined pursuant to §1274(d). The following three alternative rates are prescribed for term loans:

1. A short-term rate for loans of three years or less
2. A mid-term rate for loans over three years but not over nine years
3. A long-term rate for loans over nine years

In the case of a demand loan, the applicable federal rate will be the federal short term rate applicable for the period for which the amount of forgone interest is being determined, compounded semiannually (refer to §7872(f)(2)(B)). These rates are promulgated monthly in a revenue ruling published by the IRS.

Small Gift Loan Exception

No amount is treated as transferred by the lender to the borrower or retransferred by the borrower to the lender for any day during which the aggregate outstanding amount of loans does not exceed $10,000 (see IRC §7872(c)(2)). This small loan rule does not apply, however, if the loan is directly attributable to the purchase or carrying of income producing assets (see IRC §7872(c)(2)(B)). This exception allows small interest-free loans to children and grandchildren to help them fund short-term cash requirements, medical expense, educational expenses, and similar costs without an income and gift tax effect.

Gift Loan Interest Accrual Limitation

The amount treated as retransferred by the borrower to the lender for any day on which the aggregate amount of loans between the lender and the borrower does not exceed $100,000 is limited to the borrower's net investment income for the year (see IRC §7872(d)(1)). If the borrower has outstanding two or more gift loans, net investment income is allocated among such loans in proportion to the respective amounts that would be treated as retransferred by the borrower without regard to this limitation. If a borrower has less than $1,000 of net investment income for the year, the borrower's net investment income for the year is deemed to be zero. Accordingly, if the aggregate outstanding amount of loans from the lender to the borrower does not exceed $100,000 on any day during the year and the borrower has less than $1,000 of net investment income for the year, no amount is treated as retransferred by the borrower to the lender for said year. The objective of this provision is to enable greater flexibility to an older generation member in loaning funds without interest to a younger generation member and without the application of the §7872 imputed interest rules. For example, this could enable a loan to a child to assist the child in the purchase of a personal residence.

Sale of Property and Understated Interest

While taxpayers normally have considerable flexibility in structuring the loan terms under which they acquire a residence, this flexibility is not unlimited. The Code requires that there be adequate interest stated as to the amount of any indebtedness. There are really two aspects of the interest rate question:

1. The capital gains versus interest arbitrage
2. The bargain loan situation

In some contexts the seller and purchaser may desire to understate the interest to provide the seller a greater capital gain as to a given stream of payments. In this situation, the tax benefit of the capital gain rate is being arbitraged against the tax benefit of the interest deduction. However, if the liability is embodied in a debt instrument issued by the purchaser without adequate stated interest, then a portion of the liability may in effect be converted to interest under IRC §1274 entitled *Determination of Issue Price in The Case of Certain Debt Instruments Issued for Property* or IRC §483 entitled *Interest on Certain Deferred Payments*, and the amount of the purchaser's basis thus is reduced. As a corollary, only the principal amount remaining after application of IRC §1274 is includible in the purchaser's basis.

Note: Section 1274 does not apply to a debt instrument arising from an individual's sale or exchange of her principal residence or from sales involving total payments of $250,000 or less, but IRC §483 may apply.

Section 483 treats as interest a portion of certain deferred principal payments not subject to IRC §1274 when the rate of stated interest is inadequate. If IRC §483 applies to a debt instrument issued by a purchaser, a comparable reduction of the purchaser's basis in the property acquired takes place. The basis of the property is reduced by the portion of deferred principal treated as interest under IRC §483. Section 1274 or section 483 would apply to an assumption of an existing liability only if the terms of the liability were modified in connection with the assumption.

It should also be noted that under IRC §1274A, the usual discount rate under either IRC §483 or §1274 would be the lesser of 9 percent compounded semiannually or an *applicable federal rate* (AFR) based on the average market yield of U.S. marketable obligations.

A seller or other lender may also choose to charge a low interest rate for reasons unrelated to the capital gains rate arbitrage discussed immediately above. The most common form of this other situation is an intra-family loan. The lender could either be the seller or a third party to the purchase transaction. In either circumstance, the lender is motivated by a desire to make the financing available at a lower cost than the disinterested marketplace would provide for that same borrower, usually because of a combination of love and affection between the parties, a high tax bracket for the lender, and the fact that the lender does not particularly need the after tax cash flow that a market loan rate would provide.

Another section, IRC §7872 entitled *Treatment of Loans with Below Market Interest Rates* addresses this (refer to the discussion in the following section "Nanny Tax: Form 1040, Schedule H"). Section 7872 does not apply to any loan to which either IRC §483 or IRC §1274 applies. This includes situations where those situations would otherwise apply except for a safe harbor under those statutes. Generally, IRC §7872 does not apply to any loan in which there is *sufficient stated interest*. Sufficient stated interest exists if the loan provides for interest on the unpaid balance at the AFR appropriate for the loan. The AFR is applied differently depending on whether the loan in question is a term loan or whether it is a demand loan, (for more information, refer to the following section "Nanny Tax: Form 1040, Schedule H").

Nanny Tax: Form 1040, Schedule H.

Employers of domestic service employees must file annual returns of domestic service employment taxes on a calendar-year basis, according to IRC §3510(a)(1), on or before the 15th day of the fourth month following the close of the employer's tax year (see also IRC §3510(a)(2)). Household employers report withheld income and FICA tax for their household employees on their individual income tax return (Form 1040, Schedule H) and need employer identification numbers (EINs). EINs can be applied for on Form SS-4.

Annual Form 940 (FUTA) doesn't have to be filed for domestic employees. There is no requirement to make deposits of domestic service employment taxes or to pay installments of these taxes under IRC §6157, IRC §3510(a)(3) dealing with quarterly payment of FUTA tax.

Domestic service employment taxes are

1. any FICA and FUTA taxes on remuneration paid for domestic service in a private home of the employer (for dollar threshold see below), and

2. any income tax on these payments that is withheld under the IRC §3402(p) voluntary withholding agreement rules (see IRC §3510(c)). Withholding is not required from remuneration paid for household services performed by an employee in or about the employer's private home, provided the house is not used primarily to supply board or lodging as a business enterprise (refer to IRC §3401(a)(3), Reg §31.3401(a)(3)-1(a)(1)).

A private home is a *fixed place of abode* of an individual or family. It may include a separate and distinct dwelling unit maintained by an individual in an apartment house, hotel, or similar establishment. However, there is no exemption for services performed in or about rooming houses, lodging houses, boarding houses, clubs (except local college clubs), hotels, hospitals, eleemosynary institutions, or commercial offices or establishments (see Reg §31.3401(a)(3)-1(a)(1), Reg §31.3401(a)(3)-1(c)).

Household services in or about a private home include those performed by cooks, waiters, butlers, housekeepers, governesses, maids, valets, babysitters, janitors, laundresses, furnacemen, caretakers, handymen, gardeners, footmen, grooms, and chauffeurs of automobiles for family use. Household services also include services performed by an individual hired to drive and maintain a bus for family use or a companion for a convalescent (see Reg §31.3401(a)(3)-1(a)(2), Rev Rul 58-580, 1958-2 CB 723, Rev Rul 56-109, 1956-1 CB 467).

Non-cash payments for domestic services in an employer's private home are excluded from FICA wages. Cash remuneration paid by an employer for domestic service in the employer's private home isn't FICA wages if the cash remuneration paid during the year is less than the *applicable dollar threshold*—$1,500 in 2006 and 2007 (see IRC §3121(a)(7); IRC §3121(x)). The dollar threshold applies separately to each domestic employee. Thus, if an employer pays $1,450 each to a babysitter and a housekeeper in 2006, no FICA tax is due for either.

An employer must furnish Form W-2 to household employees whose wages are subject to Social Security taxes even if they aren't subject to income tax withholding (see Reg §31.6051-1(b)(1)). Use a Form W-3 transmittal to file even one Form W-2.

The Future of Long-Term Care Planning

11

With Medicaid costs swallowing state government budgets and the bulge in U.S. demographics that is the Baby Boomers now beginning to hit retirement age, many predict a long-term care train wreck in our future. More people will need more care than they can afford and our federal and state governments will not be able to afford to fill the gap.

The so-called "dependency ratio" of those 65 and older (mostly not working) to those 20-64 (mostly working) has hovered around 20 percent since 1985. However, it is expected to shoot up to 35 percent by 2030 and to keep rising after that. The real pain in terms of costs of care will come after 2030 as the Baby Boomers move from their early retirement, the so-called "Golden Years," to the post-retirement period when they will be much more likely to be frail, ill, and in need of care.

Solutions and Problems Ahead

There is good news and bad news about the care now available and being developed. The good news is that new ways of giving care are constantly being developed. Now, only the most frail or ill seniors are moving to nursing homes. Others, if they can, are choosing newer options, including assisted living facilities and continuing care retirement communities. Both private and public entities are expanding the availability of services at home.

And technology is being developed to make people safer at home. Beginning with the lifeline services that permit frail seniors to call for help simply by pushing a button on a device they wear around their necks, new products include on-line video monitors, automatic pill dispensers, and sensors to track movement (or the lack of it) in the home. Specialists are also retrofitting homes to make them more accessible for people of all ages with disabilities.

The bad news about these new types of care is that they are extremely fragmented. There is a mix of private and public solutions of variable quality and accessibility. It is very difficult for the consumer, often in a state of crisis, to find and choose from among the available services.

Similarly medical developments have their good and bad sides. More medicine is able to keep humans alive longer. But humans often survive in a reduced state where they need more care. The Holy Grail, of course, is a cure for some of the most debilitating illnesses, such as Alzheimer's and Parkinson's diseases. If medical science can achieve breakthroughs in the treatment of these diseases, the coming long-term care bomb may be defused.

What to Advise Clients

While political leaders could take steps to improve both the quality of the services available to frail seniors and their financing, such as universal long-term care insurance through the Medicare system, the prospects for such an initiative are quite slim. That is why advice from elder law attorneys, financial planners, and accountants is so important to clients. If no public policy solution is on the horizon, individuals will have to create their own solutions. Here are a few solutions you can tell your client:

- **Earn and Save.** Earn and save enough money to pay for whatever care needs you may have. Unfortunately, few Americans can reliably reach this goal. While many can afford a year or two of care, what will they do if they need ten years of care?
- **Buy Long-Term Care Insurance.** While the long-term care industry has had its problems, which are described in Chapter 6, "Long-Term Care Insurance," it is still the best solution available for many clients. You just have to make sure that you can afford the premiums indefinitely and you must purchase the policy when you are still healthy enough to be insurable.
- **Consider a Continuing Care Retirement Community.** If you are healthy enough and affluent enough to move to a community committed to caring for you whatever your needs may be, then your will have the long-term care risk covered.

- **Consider Moving.** Move to a lower-cost part of the country or to another country altogether. The cost of living and the costs of receiving care are much higher in some parts of the country than in others. Moving to a lower-cost part of the country while you are healthy will allow you to save more money for future needs (or to pay long-term care insurance premiums) and lower the cost of care when and if you need it. You may be able to save even more money and improve your standard of living by moving to another country entirely, such as Mexico or Costa Rica.

- **Plan for Medicaid Coverage.** If none of the above options are available to you, you can plan to protect your home and savings and qualify for Medicaid to cover your cost of care. This approach, however, has drawbacks. While Medicaid covers nursing home care in most states, its coverage of home and assisted living care is much less available, limiting your options. In addition, most planning techniques involve transferring assets to children or into trust. Transfers to children put the parent in a vulnerable and dependent position, depending on the child for financial assistance when and if the parent runs out of funds. Transfers into trust limit the availability of the assets in trust for the senior's use.

- **Plan for Flexibility.** Since the future is unknown, it is important that clients be able to react and make changes depending on changes in their health, in the law, in living circumstances, and in the availability of services. Every client should have a durable power of attorney, a health care directive, and a revocable trust.

- **Don't Plan.** If a client cannot take any of the steps suggested above, other than the minimal estate planning described in the preceding paragraph, taking no long-term care planning steps is not necessarily fatal. The difficulty in planning ahead is that the future is not yet known. The advantage of not planning and simply living one's life to the fullest is that planning steps may be taken when the future arrives. Then we know what our health is, what the laws are, and what options are available. It's never too late to do some planning. While the options may be more limited, they also may be clearer. And if the client has a durable power of attorney, a health care directive, and a revocable trust, it won't be too late to act.

Conclusion

Long-term care planning, a growing concern and practice area over the past 20 years, is going to keep growing as the Baby Boomers age. Clients will need the assistance of all of their advisors in planning for their future. And all of their advisors need to work together as a team to provide the best solution for each client.

Glossary[1]

The following glossary is made up of selections from the *Dictionary of Eldercare Terminology*, 2nd edition, by Walter Feldesman.

Activities of Daily Living (ADL). Activities usually performed for oneself in the course of a normal day. Although definitions differ, ADLs are usually considered to be mobility (for example, transfer from bed to chair), dressing, bathing, self-feeding, and toileting.

People may need assistance with ADLs regardless of their living arrangements. Assistance to a person limited in his ADLs is customarily performed by a family member, a home health aide or attendant, or a nurse's aide in a nursing facility. The assistance is of a nonmedical nature, commonly characterized as personal care, custodial care, or physical care. Assistance provided in a home setting may extend beyond ADLs and includes such nonmedical activities as housekeeping (for example, cleaning and cooking), laundry, and shopping.

Medicare cannot be looked to, except to a limited extent, for coverage of assistance with ADLs. Medicare pays for acute care services and does not provide coverage for chronic personal or custodial care.

Medicaid, unlike Medicare, will cover Medicaid-eligible persons for many home care services including personal care, and, in certain cases, ancillary services such as housekeeping.

---

[1] Copyright © by National Information Services Corporation, 3100 St. Paul Street, Baltimore, MD 21218; Telephone: 1-410-243-0797; Web site: www.nisc.com.

It is available from National Information Services Corporation (Baltimore, MD). The entire dictionary is available for $28.00 + $6.50 S&H and can be ordered on-line from http://www.nisc.com/Frame/NISC_products-f.htm.

Dennis Haber of Senior Funding Group, 247 West Old Country Road, Hicksville, NY 11801; Telephone: 1-516-570-5400 x208; Cell: 1-516-551-2189; E-mail: denhaber@aol.com also contributed to this glossary.

Adult Guardian. The person appointed by a court, usually a probate court under a modern protective services statute, to perform the court-ordered tasks of caring for an incapacitated adult's financial affairs, personal needs, or both. The following three different types of guardians have varying degrees of authority:

- **Plenary guardian.** Has total authority over personal and property matters
- **Guardian of the person.** Has authority only over personal matters such as medical decisions and residential questions
- **Guardian of the estate.** Has authority over property only

Assisted Living Facility. Provides a combination of housing and personalized health care in a professionally managed group-living environment designed to respond to the individual needs of persons who require assistance with activities of daily living.

This type of facility is specifically designed to promote maximum independence and dignity in the most residential and homelike setting possible. It may be all or part of a building that houses a few or several hundred persons, or a distinct part of a residential campus. It traditionally serves the frailer resident who cannot or chooses not to live alone, but who does not require the 24-hour skilled or custodial care of a nursing home.

Generally, residents of this type of housing pay privately in the form of rent, rent plus service charge, and sometimes a deposit or entry fee. In some states, Medicaid will pay for certain ADL services under home and community-based service waivers. Medicaid will not pay for room and board charges. Private long-term care insurance may also be used for some of the provided services.

Licensure of this housing type varies by state, depending upon each state's own regulatory requirements. These facilities sometimes are called residential care homes, domiciliary care homes, personal care homes, adult congregate living facilities, homes for the aged, catered living facilities, or board and care homes.

Balance Billing/Medicare. This term refers to health care providers charging patients for amounts above the Medicare-approved charge. By Federal law antedating the Balanced Budget Act of 1997, the maximum allowable charge (charge limit) may not exceed 115% of the Medicare-approved charge. A number of states—Connecticut, Massachusetts, Minnesota, New York, Ohio, Pennsylvania, Rhode Island, and Vermont—have by state statute banned the practice of balance billing. Although the statutes have been challenged in Federal courts on preemption grounds, each has withstood the challenge.

Under the Balanced Budget Act of 1997 that created Medicare+ Choice plans, health care providers may or may not be permitted to engage in the practice of balance billing—depending upon the type of plan and whether or not the provider has a contract with the plan.

- **Providers under contract.** Under all Medicare+Choice plans, except private fee-for-service (PFFS) plans, physicians and other health care providers who contract with a plan may not balance bill. However, a contracting physician or other health care provider under a PFFS contract that establishes a payment rate for services may balance bill (that is, charge) for their services an amount not to exceed, including deductibles, coinsurance, copayments, or other balance billing, 115% of such payment rate.

- **Providers not under contract.** Under all Medicare+Choice plans, except Medicare+Choice medical savings accounts (MSA) and PFFS plans, noncontracting physicians or other health care providers may not balance bill, but must accept as payment in full from a Medicare+Choice plan enrollee the amount that would have been paid under traditional Medicare fee-for-service arrangement. However, a noncontracting physician or other health provider under an MSA or PFFS plan may balance bill without limitation.

Bed hold/Medicaid, Medicare. Preservation of a nursing home bed when a nursing home resident is temporarily hospitalized or out of the facility on therapeutic leave. State Medicaid programs may pay for bed holds, but are not required to. Nursing facility residents on Medicaid have a right to return to the first available bed in the facility that they temporarily left, even if the state has not paid to hold their original bed.

Medicare does not itself pay to hold a bed; moreover, it prohibits facilities from taking payment from beneficiaries to hold a bed if the date of return is certain. If it is not certain, beneficiaries may pay.

Community Spouse's Resource Allowance (CSRA)/Medicaid. The CSRA is an amount of resources that states must protect for the spouse of an institutionalized person seeking Medicaid coverage. It is determined by application of a formula, or, as explained below, through a fair hearing or by court order. The CSRA may not be counted in determining the eligibility of an individual seeking Medicaid.

The CSRA is determined as follows:

1. All nonexempt resources belonging to either member of the married couple will be pooled together regardless of who owns them and regardless of marital property laws (for example, equitable distribution laws or community property laws).
2. The community spouse is entitled to an amount (community resource allowance), subject to paragraph 3 below, between $20,880 and $104,400 in 2008.
3. A state may establish a dollar amount that is both the minimum and maximum resource amount. Under the foregoing formula, $104,400 represents a maximum and $20,880 represents a minimum on the CSRA. A state, by opting to use the maximum resource amount, can establish $104,400 as both a maximum and minimum. A state may opt to select a spousal share amount that, in the alternative, is that sum or a greater figure equal to one-half of the couple's resources, but not to exceed the maximum figure of $104,400.
4. The CSRA amount is determined according to resources owned by the couple on the first day of a continuous period of institutionalization regardless of whether the institutionalized spouse applied for Medicaid at the time. Either spouse may ask the Medicaid agency to complete an assessment of their resources as of that time. The CSRA can be increased above the formula amount in two ways:

   - Either spouse can request a fair hearing in which to demonstrate that a larger amount of resources must be protected (that is, transferred to the community spouse from the institutionalized spouse) to generate income needed to bring the community spouse's income up to the minimum monthly maintenance needs allowance.
   - A court order granting a larger amount of resources for the community spouse; the order must be honored by the Medicaid agency.

Continuing Care Retirement Community (CCRC). This type of housing alternative, sometimes called a life care community, generally requires that an individual be able to live independently upon becoming a resident in the community. As a resident begins to need more assistance, specific additional services are made available. Most CCRCs offer three basic levels of housing on an as-needed basis: fully independent living, assisted living (personal care services), and skilled nursing care.

The basic idea of a CCRC is that once an individual becomes a resident, he never has to move again because any housing type and personal care services he will probably ever need are provided within the single campus setting. A CCRC guarantees housing and care across the continuum in that one community.

Generally, a CCRC will charge an entrance fee as well as a monthly payment for its residential, leisure, and nursing services. In some cases, health care and personal care services can be paid for on an as-needed basis. The entrance fee, formerly nonrefundable, now is generally refundable on departure under a variety of specified conditions.

Basically, there are three types of CCRC contracts:

- **Extensive contract.** Covers shelter and residential services, amenities (for example, swimming pools, tennis courts, and other types of recreation facilities), and unlimited long-term nursing care. The entrance fees and the monthly costs are usually higher than those under modified or fee-for-service contracts.
- **Modified or fee-for-service contract.** Provides shelter, residential services, and amenities, plus a specified amount of nursing care, which the resident can obtain on an unlimited basis provided he pays for it at a daily or monthly nursing care rate.
- **Fee-for-service continuing care contract.** Covers shelter, meals, residential services and amenities, and, in addition, emergency and short-term nursing care. Access to long-term nursing care is provided only upon a daily nursing care rate.

Discharge Planning. This service is usually performed by a social worker on staff in connection with a discharge of a patient from a hospital, nursing home, or like institution. Discharge planning involves the social worker assessing the patient's level of functioning and needs following his discharge, including a smooth transition in moving from one level of care to another (for example, from a hospital to a nursing home or from a hospital to home care). The discharge planner also contacts home health agencies to assist the patient in connection with his home care.

Estate Recovery/Medicaid. Federal law mandates that each state place into effect an estate recovery program that provides for recovery of medical assistance to a Medicaid recipient. Mandated recovery centers mostly around the receipt by chronically ill individuals of long-term care services, although states may opt to recover Medicaid payments for other services rendered. The individuals and the assets subject to mandated recovery are set forth in the following list.

1. **Individuals subject to recovery.** Recovery must be sought by the state from the following three categories of persons:

    a) **Permanently institutionalized individuals.** These are individuals in nursing facilities, intermediate care facilities for the mentally retarded, or other medical institutions where the state has determined that the individual cannot reasonably be discharged from the facility and return home.

    b) **Individuals age 55 and over.** These individuals received from the state, through Medicaid, nursing home facility care, home and community-based services, and related hospital and prescription drug services.

    c) **Individuals with certain state authorized insurance programs.** These individuals received Medicaid assistance under provisions of a state law (not recognized by Medicaid law) that permits a disregard by Medicaid of assets because of purchase of long-term care insurance, which is known as a Robert Wood Johnson Foundation insurance plan. Exempted are those individuals in five states with such state laws that are recognized by Medicaid law, which were in effect on May 14, 1993. These states are California, Connecticut, Indiana, Iowa, and New York.

2. **Assets subject to recovery.** The assets of these three categories of individuals that are subject to state recovery are set forth in the following list.

    a) Recovery must be sought from the estates of these individuals, as the term is defined by state probate law. States may adopt a broader definition of estate than is defined in state probate laws to include jointly held property and other property in which the recipient had a legal interest at the time of death. All states, except the five states mentioned in section 1c above, are mandated to apply this broader definition to any individual who received Medicaid nursing facility and other long-term care services under a Robert Wood Johnson insurance plan.

b) Recovery cannot occur against an individual's assets until after the death of the surviving spouse and until there are no blind or disabled children or children under age 21.

c) If a lien has been properly imposed upon a Medicaid recipient's homestead, the state must seek recovery upon the sale of the liened property or from the estate of the recipient after he dies. In either case, the state may not seek recovery if the Medicaid recipient's spouse is alive, if blind or disabled children or children under age 21 are alive, or if certain siblings or caretaker children reside in the house.

d) Recovery from a spouse who survived the Medicaid recipient is neither required nor authorized by Medicaid law. However, some state laws do authorize recovery from a surviving spouse's estate, though these laws have been challenged as being beyond the scope of and inconsistent with the Federal law.

In situations where recovery would cause undue hardship, Federal law requires states to waive it.

Expected Interest Rate. The expected interest rate has only one function—to help determine how much money your client can get. The expected interest rate is based upon the yield on the ten-year treasury plus a margin. (At some point in the future, the expected interest rate will be based upon the ten-year swap rate for those programs using the LIBOR [London Interbank Offered Rate] index.) When the expected interest rate goes up, the principal limit goes down. When the expected interest rate goes down, the principal limit goes up. This characteristic can cause a lot of fear because a reverse mortgage borrower would never know just how much money he would receive because of this see-saw effect until he starts the process.

Since 2003, the principal limit is protected if the closing occurs within the prescribed period of time. A borrower is protected from getting fewer funds if, at the time of closing, the expected interest rate is higher than at the time of application. On the other hand, the borrower will have access to more funds if the expected interest rate is lower than it was at the time the application was taken.

FHA Lending Limit. This amount usually changes each year. Every county in the country has such a limit. This amount can differ greatly from county to county. For example, at the time of this writing, the FHA lending limit in some counties in New York is $362,790. This means that if a borrower lives in a $450,000 home, $362,790 of the $450,000 home is counted toward determining how much money he can get. Your client will maximize what he can get from a value perspective if the value of the home equals at least the lending limit in his area. A value greater than the lending limit will not enable a borrower to get more money. On the other hand, a lesser value will decrease how much money a client can get. So as your client considers a reverse mortgage, you should find out what the FHA lending limit is in his area. Should congress pass the FHA Modernization Bill, there could soon be a single national loan limit.

HECM loan. Whether you are referring to a U.S. Department of Housing and Urban Development (HUD), Federal Housing Administration (FHA), or Home Equity Conversion Mortgage (HECM), you are referring to the same type of government insured loan. A proprietary loan refers to the Federal National Mortgage Association loan. A private proprietary loan refers to a nongovernment insured loan. These loans are partially modeled after the HECM.

Hospice Care/Medicare. Hospice care is designed for terminally ill persons and is covered by Medicare Part A. Hospice programs will care for patients in a hospice facility or whenever possible in their homes and emphasize relieving pain and managing symptoms rather than undertaking curative procedures. An individual may elect to receive hospice care rather than regular Medicare benefits for the management of his illness. For routine home care, Medicare coverage is available for the level of care that is reasonable and necessary. For periods of crisis, Medicare will cover continuous home care, including nursing for up to 24 hours per day. The beneficiary need not be homebound. During a person's lifetime, Medicare pays for up to two 90-day periods of hospice care followed by an unlimited number of 60-day periods from which the individual elects to receive hospice, provided the following four conditions are met:

- The attending physician—either in the employ of the hospice or under contract with the hospice as an independent physician or as part of an independent physician's group—and the medical director of the hospice must establish and periodically review a written plan for hospice care, and, at the beginning of each of the successive periods mentioned above, certify that a patient is terminally ill (that is, that the patient's life expectancy is six months or less.
- The patient must elect to receive care from a hospice instead of from standard Medicare medical benefits for the terminal illness. A patient may elect to revert to standard Medicare benefits, but he will then be required to pay any applicable deductibles and copayments.
- Care must be provided by a Medicare-certified hospice program.
- The individual must be eligible for Part A benefits.

If these conditions are met, Medicare will pay for the following services:

- nursing services
- doctors' services
- drugs, including outpatient drugs for pain relief and symptom management
- physical, occupational, and speech-language therapy
- home health aides and homemaker services
- medical social services
- medical supplies (including drugs and biologicals) and appliances
- short-term inpatient care including respite care, procedures necessary for pain control, and acute and chronic symptom management
- training and counseling for the patient and family members
- any other item or service that is specified in the plan mentioned above and for which payment may otherwise by paid by Medicare

There is no deductible for these hospice care benefits. Copayments, however, are required for two benefits:

- prescription drugs for pain relief and symptom management, for which patients can be charged 5% of the reasonable cost, but no more than $5 per prescription
- respite care, for which a patient can be charged about $5 per day, depending on the area of the country

Medicare+Choice organizations are not required to provide hospice services but may do so on a voluntary basis

Income Cap States/Medicaid. Several states, referred to as income cap states, do not have a medically needy program serving nursing facility residents. In these states, individuals are not allowed to spend down to the supplemental security income (SSI) income level (that is, cap) to become eligible for Medicaid-covered nursing home care.

These states avail themselves of an optional Medicaid program termed the *optional categorically needy program* under which individuals are provided limited nursing facility coverage. Under this program, individuals qualify for Medicaid nursing home coverage if their countable income does not exceed a cap of a prescribed percentage, usually 300%, of the SSI benefit for one person. The cap is categorically fixed and severe: one dollar of excess income above the cap will disqualify the individual. An individual is not permitted to spend down for medical expenses, nor can he forego collection of a pension, Social Security benefits, or interest income in order to fall within the income cap.

A possible method for reducing the income of an individual seeking to qualify under the optional categorically needy program, also commonly referred to as the 300% program, is to obtain from a state court a *qualified domestic relations order* that allocates pension payments to the community spouse. The community spouse as the payee under such order arguably is the beneficiary of the pension, and payments to him would constitute his income under the name-on-the-check rule, not income of the institutionalized spouse who was the original pensioner.

Another method of qualifying for the optional categorically needy program is available under the provisions of Omnibus Budget Reallocation Act of 1993. With this law, Congress allowed individuals in income cap states to become eligible for Medicaid nursing home assistance by putting their income (for example, pensions or Social Security benefits) into a so-called Miller trust. During the Medicaid recipient's lifetime, all but a small portion of the money in the trust must go toward paying the nursing home bill. If any money remains in the trust after the recipient's death, it must be paid to the state, up to the amount of Medicaid assistance that was rendered.

The income cap states are Alabama, Alaska, Colorado, Delaware, Idaho, Mississippi, Nevada, New Mexico, Ohio, South Dakota, and Wyoming.

Initial Interest Rate. Think of this as the *note rate*. Every loan contains an interest rate. The adjustable interest rate can adjust on a monthly basis or annual basis. As of this writing, the lowest constant maturity treasury (CMT) index margin on the monthly adjustable is 1. The margin on the yearly adjustable is 3.1. The fixed rate reverse mortgage program that exists as of this writing uses a combination of the yield on the ten-year treasury and the five-year swap rate to determine the interest rate. The LIBOR index will in time replace the CMT index as the preferred adjustable rate index.

Line of Credit (LOC). A reverse mortgage line of credit option is significantly different than a typical line of credit. Let's say that you have a $200,000 letter of credit (LOC) from your neighborhood bank. You have not used the line for two years. How much would you have in the LOC? The answer is the same $200,000. Now let's pose the same question regarding the reverse mortgage LOC. How much money would you have in the line after two years? The answer is an amount greater than the $200,000. The line contains a growth factor that increases the amount one can borrow. (Actually, the credit or principal limit is growing). This growth factor has no income tax implications as it simply increases the amount one can borrow on their reverse mortgage loan, but not all reverse mortgage programs provide a growth factor in their LOC.

Nursing Home Reform Law. Sometimes referred to as OBRA '87, this Federal law regulating aspects of nursing homes is contained in the Omnibus Budget Reconciliation Act of 1987. It is the most comprehensive Federal nursing home law since the passage of Medicare and Medicaid in 1965. It sets Federal standards of care, including one stipulating that nursing homes may use physical and chemical restraints only in very specific circumstances and only after other interventions have been tried. The bill also establishes certain rights for patients and requires states and the Federal government to inspect nursing homes and enforce standards through the use of a range of sanctions designed to promote compliance without forcing the relocation of residents due to the closing of facilities.

The resident's bill of rights, mandated in the nursing home reform law, includes a resident's right to

- admit and discharge oneself;
- control one's own medical care and be informed of all aspects of one's health;

- choose his own physician of own choice and refuse treatment;
- self-administer drugs;
- be free of restraints (physical or chemical);
- see all his medical records;
- receive notice of any decision to transfer or discharge or change a roommate;
- manage own financial affairs;
- receive visitors of one's choice as well as refuse visitors; and
- have access to a private telephone.

Transfers or discharges are permitted only under the following three situations:

- If it is necessary for the resident's welfare and if his needs cannot be met in the facility
- If a resident's health has improved and he no longer needs care
- If a resident's presence or nonpayment of charges endangers the health and safety of other residents in the facility

All residents, whether paying privately or receiving Medicaid assistance or Medicare benefits, are entitled to due process (namely, a fair hearing). In this connection, the procedures for Medicaid fair hearings apply to nursing home transfers and discharges. The right to a pre-transfer hearing is mandated except for emergency transfers subject to a resident's right to a bed hold pending a post-transfer hearing.

The law requires every resident to undergo a process known as pre-admission, screening, and annual resident review. Prior to admission, there is to be a functional evaluation and, at the time of admission, a comprehensive care plan must be developed. This plan must be prepared annually with a physician and nursing team.

The law contains a number of other significant requirements. Nursing homes may not require as a condition for admission or for continuing stay a guarantee of payment from a third party. They must provide coverage by a registered nurse no less than eight hours a day, seven days a week. Aides must go through a training program and pass a nursing aide registry certification. States are required to create a nursing aide registry to train, certify, and maintain a listing of all approved workers.

Pourover Will. The testator provides in his will that designated assets will be paid over and distributed to a previously established trust.

Principal Limit. The gross amount a client can borrow based upon the age of the youngest borrower, value of the home (up to the FHA lending limit in your county), and the expected interest rate. It is from a principal limit that items get deducted to arrive at the net amount a client can use for himself after considering closing costs, service set aside, and liens that need to be paid off.

Program for All-Inclusive Care for the Elderly (PACE). Based on a model created by On Lok Senior Services in San Francisco, this program began as a Medicare and Medicaid demonstration project initially tested at ten sites. The Balanced Budget Act expanded PACE to become an option open to all states. PACE targets frail elderly persons living at home who are eligible for nursing home care. The program integrates health and long-term care services in an adult day care setting and uses a multidisciplinary case management team of providers, including physicians, nurses, social workers, nutritionists, occupational and speech therapists, and health and transportation personnel. PACE participants are required to attend an adult day care center regularly.

Unlike the Social Health Maintenance Organization project, PACE providers in the demonstration project receive most of their funding from Medicaid. The funding is allocated according to a fixed monthly capitated fee for each participant based on the frailty of enrollees. The project represents a test to link acute care under Medicare and long-term care under Medicaid.

The Balanced Budget Act of 1997 established PACE as a state option to furnish comprehensive health care to persons who are enrolled with an organization that has contracted to operate the PACE program, who are eligible for Medicaid, and who receive Medicaid solely through the PACE program. The salient characteristics of PACE offered as a state option are set forth below.

PACE providers may be public or private not-for-profit entities, except for those entities (up to ten) participating in the demonstration to test the operation of PACE by private, for-profit entities. During the three-year period beginning August 5, 1997, the Secretary of Health and Human Services (HHS) is required to give priority to entities operating a PACE demonstration waiver program and then to entities that have applied to operate a program as of May 1, 1997. The number of PACE program agreements that may be effective on August 5 of each year is limited. Health Care Financing Administration (HCFA) authorized up to 80 in 1999 and has limited increases by 20 for each following year.

Persons eligible for PACE must be 55 years of age or older; require nursing facility level of care that would be covered under a state's Medicaid program; reside in the service area of the PACE program; and meet such other eligibility conditions as may be imposed under the PACE program agreement. Eligible individuals include both Medicare and Medicaid beneficiaries. Medicare participants not enrolled in the PACE program through Medicaid must pay premiums equal to Medicaid capitation. PACE enrollees will be reevaluated annually to determine if they continue to need nursing facility level of care.

Under a PACE agreement, a provider at a minimum must provide eligible persons all care and services covered under Medicare and Medicaid. The services must be provided without any limitation or condition as to amount, duration, and scope and without application of deductibles, copayments, coinsurance, or other cost sharing that would otherwise apply under Medicare or Medicaid. The services must be provided 24 hours per day, every day of the year through a comprehensive multi-disciplinary health and social services delivery system that integrates acute and long-term services.

Primary medical care for a PACE enrollee must be furnished by a primary care physician who serves as a gatekeeper for access to treatment by specialists. HCFA may grant waivers of this requirement. A primary care physician, registered nurse, medical director, program director, other health professionals, and a governing body to guide the operation must be part of the multi-disciplinary team.

States will make a prospective monthly capitation payment for each enrollee in an amount specified in the PACE agreement. PACE agreements are for one year, but may be extended for additional contract years at the discretion of the Secretary of HHS.

Qualified Long-Term Care Insurance Contract. The Health Insurance Portability and Accountability Act of 1996 extends certain tax advantages to a qualified long-term care insurance (LTCI) contract, sometimes informally called a tax-qualified policy. The law defines such a contract as a guaranteed renewable life insurance contract or as a rider to a life insurance contract, under which the only insurance protection provided is coverage of qualified long-term care services. A qualified LTCI contract does not pay or reimburse expenses reimbursable by Medicare (except for coinsurance or deductible amounts) nor does it provide for a cash surrender value or other money that can be paid, pledged or borrowed. Further, certain consumer protection provisions set forth in the Long-term Care Services Model Regulations and Model Act of the National Association of Insurance Commissioners must be part of the contract.

To be qualified, LTCI contracts sold after January 1, 1997, must meet these Federal standards. Policies issued prior to this date that have met existing state standards are considered qualified policies, though they may not meet the Federal requirements.

Qualified Long-term Care Services. The Health Insurance Portability and Accountability Act of 1996 defines qualified long-term services as necessary diagnostic, preventive, therapeutic, curing, treating, mitigating and rehabilitative services, and maintenance or personal care services that are required by a chronically ill individual and provided pursuant to a plan of care prescribed by a licensed health care provider. The phrase *maintenance or personal care services* means any care the primary purpose of which is the provision of needed assistance with any of the disabilities as a result of which the individual is chronically ill, including severe cognitive impairment. The cost of qualified long-term services can be counted as a medical expense deduction for income tax purposes.

Remainderman. This is a person or other entity designated in a trust as the beneficiary entitled to the principal or corpus of the trust after the income-paying stage comes to an end (that is, after the income beneficiary of the trust has been paid in full in accordance with the terms of the trust).

Representative Payee. Under Federal laws a representative payee may act as a surrogate on behalf of an individual who is not capable of making cognitive decisions, for the purpose of receiving and handling cash benefit checks of a Social Security or SSI recipient. The legal authority of the surrogate is usually limited to merely managing the benefits received for the well-being of the original beneficiary. A representative payee can be a public agency, nonprofit organization, bank, or an individual.

The designation of a representative payee generally is a protective arrangement for incapacitated persons. It is less restrictive, simpler, and less expensive than alternative protective arrangements such as guardianship or conservatorship and does not require a judicial finding of incompetency or incapacity. The arrangement can be terminated if the recipient regains cognitive ability to handle the government benefits to which he is entitled.

Reverse Mortgage. A reverse equity mortgage allows senior citizens who are house rich and cash poor to obtain a loan based on the equity in their home. They retain title to their home as long as they continue to live there and receive nontaxable income that they can flexibly use for their own needs. According to the terms of most mortgages currently available, the loan, interest, and other costs such as origination fees do not have to be paid back until the owner vacates the property through a move or death. Almost all reverse mortgages now provide a guarantee of lifetime tenancy. Most reverse mortgages are non-recourse loans, which means the lender can look only to the value of the home for repayment.

Payments to a homeowner from a reverse mortgage can be in the form of a single lump sum of cash, regular monthly advances, or a line of credit. New mortgage plans allow a combination of payment methods. The amount of the loan is seldom for the full value of the property; most lenders place minimum and maximum limits on the size of mortgages they are willing to establish. Loan periods can vary.

Some mortgages combine a reverse mortgage with an annuity, thereby guaranteeing individuals monthly income for their lifetimes regardless of whether they continue to live in their homes or not. The monthly payments are considered annuity advances and, thus, partially taxable. For purposes of Medicaid eligibility, these payments may be counted as income.

Reverse mortgages are currently available in all states, except Texas and the District of Columbia. Several different plans are available—some more widely than others. Plan features offered by the same lender can vary from state to state. The HECM is federally insured through HUD and is the most widely available plan. In 1995, the Federal National Mortgage Association began a program called Home Keeper. The three main private for-profit plans are offered by Transamerica HomeFirst, Freedom House Equity Partners, and Household Senior Services.

Roth IRA. The Roth IRA, named after Senator Roth who created it under the Taxpayer Relief Act of 1997, is a nondeductible individual retirement account. Several significant differences exist between a traditional or deductible IRA and a Roth IRA:

- Eligibility to contribute to a Roth IRA is subject to special adjusted gross income limits.
- Contributions to a Roth IRA are not deductible.
- Roth IRA contributions may be made after the owner has attained the age of 70$\frac{1}{2}$.
- Qualified distributions from a Roth IRA are not included in gross income or subject to the minimum distribution rules if certain conditions are met.

As with a traditional IRA, the income earned on the assets of a Roth IRA is tax free prior to distribution. Contributions to a Roth IRA are subject to two limitations:

- **Dollar limitation.** Under this, a contribution cannot exceed the maximum amount allowed after the deduction for a regular IRA (the lesser of $5,000, $6,000 for age 50 and above, or 100% of an individual's compensation) nor can it be reduced by any contributions that an individual may have made for a taxable year to any other individual retirement plan(s) maintained for the individual's benefit.
- **Adjusted gross income limitation.** This is based upon an individual's modified adjusted gross income. The Roth IRA contribution for a taxable year is phased out after adjusted gross income reaches certain levels. The amount an individual can contribute to a Roth IRA declines when his income reaches $95,000 and phases out entirely when the adjusted gross income reaches $110,000. For married individuals filing jointly, the phase out occurs when their adjusted gross income is between $150,000 and $160,000, and for married individuals filing separately, the phase out occurs when the adjusted gross income is between $0 and $10,000.

An individual may make a regular contribution to both a traditional IRA and a Roth IRA for a taxable year. In this case, a maximum contribution limit for a Roth IRA is the lesser of the amount determined under the dollar limitation reduced by the amount contributed to a traditional IRA for the taxable year or the amount determined under the adjusted gross income limitation. Eligible taxpayers may contribute to both a Roth IRA and a deductible IRA by dividing their contribution between the two, but in no event may an individual's combined total annual contributions exceed $5,000 ($6,000 for age 50 and above).

Withdrawals from a Roth IRA are tax exempt only if the account has been in existence for at least five years and the taxpayer is at least age 59$^1/_2$ or disabled or a distribution of no more than $10,000 is made to finance the first-time home-buying expenses of a taxpayer, his spouse, children, grandchildren, or ancestors of a taxpayer or spouse.

Service Set Aside. The amount assumed to be needed to pay the accumulated servicing fees over the life of the loan. Since the borrower does not make mortgage payments, this fee gets deducted off the top. The service set aside is subtracted from the principal limit. In reality, the service set aside is a calculated amount based on age and life expectancy that is deducted from the principal limit. No amount is actually set aside. It merely represents an additional small amount of equity that will not be converted into reverse mortgage proceeds.

Skilled Nursing Care. The term refers to a level of care that must be furnished by or under direct supervision of licensed nursing personnel and under the general direction of a physician in order to assure the safety of the patient and achieve the medically desired result. The service involves observation and assessment of the total needs of the patient, planning and management of a treatment plan, and rendering direct services to the patient. As long as a patient needs skilled nursing care, it makes no difference whether his condition is acute, chronic, or terminal.

Examples of skilled nursing care are

- intravenous injections;
- tube feeding;
- kidney dialysis;
- colostomy care;
- the use of medical gases;
- observation and monitoring of a patient's unstable condition; and
- changing sterile dressings.

Expressly excluded from the term is any service that could be safely and effectively performed (or self-administered) by the average nonmedical personnel without the direct supervision of a licensed nurse.

In determining whether the level of care required by a patient is custodial care (which is not Medicare-covered) or skilled nursing care (which is covered by Medicare), the courts have applied several accepted legal principles:

- The primary responsibility determining a patient's need for skilled nursing care rests with the physician.
- While the opinion of a physician about the need for skilled nursing care is not binding with Medicare, when there is no conflicting evidence, his decision is required to give the level for care's need great weight.
- The courts will avoid using a technical approach and instead use a common sense meaning and a consideration of the needs and underlying conditions affecting the patient as a whole.

Skilled Nursing Facility/Medicare. A skilled nursing facility is specially staffed and equipped to provide intensive nursing and rehabilitative care to patients. Care is provided by registered and other licensed nurses or licensed therapists under the supervision of a doctor. Medicare's requirement for admission to a skilled nursing facility, the benefits covered, and the period of coverage are set forth in the previous definition.

Supplemental Needs Trust. This type of trust, also known as a special needs trust, is an irrevocable trust, sometimes funded by assets of a third party, created for a disabled beneficiary, and intended to supplement government benefits. The trust prohibits the trustee from spending trust assets in diminution of government benefits. The beneficiary has no power to control distributions.

For SSI and generally for Medicaid, disbursements from the trust are governed by SSI income principles. If payments are made for food, clothing, or shelter, or if payments are made directly to the beneficiary, the amounts are counted as income to the beneficiary for purposes of eligibility. The more common arrangement with such trusts is for the trustee to make direct payments to vendors of services or goods that are not food, clothing, or shelter; such payments are not considered income to the beneficiary.

In addition to these general rules, Medicaid has special rules governing the treatment of trusts established by and for a Medicaid recipient or his spouse during their lifetimes.

Tenure Payment. A Tenure payment is a monthly payment option that will never stop as long as a borrower is in the home using it as a primary residence. Think of this type of monthly payment as a bucket that can never be emptied.

Term Payment. A term payment is a monthly payment option that will stop after a period of time has expired. The amount selected to be received is in an amount greater than the tenure payment option. Think of this as a bucket that will become empty after a certain period of time has passed.

Terminally Ill. An illness, disease, or injury where recovery can no longer be reasonably expected. For purposes of Medicare-covered hospice care, a person with a terminal illness has a life expectancy of six months or less, as certified by a physician, if the illness runs a normal course. In the context of tax regulations governing accelerated benefits, a terminally ill person has a reasonable life expectancy of 24 months or less.

Testator. The person who creates a will.

Total Annual Loan Cost (TALC). This is the average interest rate that would produce the amount owed based upon a particular choice of receiving the money limited by the non-recourse feature found in reverse mortgage loans. This also includes the costs to obtain the loan.

TALC rates are usually higher in the early years because the closing costs will represent a greater percentage of the outstanding balance. As time passes and more money is accessed, the closing costs will represent a smaller portion of this outstanding balance. Therefore, these rates will be lower in later years as the balance continues to increase.

A high TALC rate usually means that there is more equity in the home. A lower TALC rate usually means that the borrower is taking a greater amount out in the early years. This means that there will be less equity in the home when the loan finally gets paid off.

TALC rates take into account the term of the loan; the payment plan and appreciation factors are merely projections.